TRANSLATION
A MEANS TO AN END

THE DOLPHIN

General Editor: Tim Caudery
Production Editor: Connie N. Relsted

18

TRANSLATION
A MEANS TO AN END

Edited by Shirley Larsen

AARHUS UNIVERSITY PRESS

General Editor: Tim Caudery
Production Editor: Connie N. Relsted

Editorial address:
The Dolphin
Department of English, Aarhus University
DK-8000 Aarhus C

Distribution:
Aarhus University Press
Building 170, Aarhus University
DK-8000 Aarhus C

ISSN 0106-4487
The Dolphin no. 18, spring issue 1990
Subscription price for one year (two issues):
Europe 198 DKK, overseas US$ 38.00.
Single copy price (not including postage):
Europe 118 DKK, overseas US$ 19.65.
Back issues available - list sent on request.

Contents

Preface

Most people would probably agree that translation is a means rather than an end in itself, but even as a means it is used in different ways, and for a variety of ends. The contributions to this volume discuss some of the means to some of the ends.

Two of the articles deal with the translation of literature. Viggo Hjørnager Pedersen (Copenhagen University) presents his own model for evaluating the quality of a given translation, and applies it to various renderings into English of Hans Christian Andersen's 'Den lille Havfrue'. Hanne Tang Grödal (a graduate of Aarhus University) looks at the process of translating from the point of view of the professional translator of literary texts, using her own translations of passages from works by Louise Erdrich and Marge Piercy as exemplification.

In one of his articles, Knud Sørensen (Aarhus University) considers some aspects of word formation in English and Danish, demonstrating how a contrastive approach can be helpful to the translator.

Four of the articles are concerned with translation as part of the teaching / learning / testing process. Flemming Olsen (Virum Statsskole) deals with translation at *gymnasium* level, relating it to the teaching of grammar, vocabulary and style, and comparing it with essay writing. Knud Sørensen assesses the role of translation at university level, focussing on its function as a uniting and consolidating factor in an academic course of study. Margrethe Mondahl and Knud Anker Jensen (The Copenhagen Business School) look at the way in which learners consciously process their linguistic knowledge while they are engaged in a translation exercise, and discuss the pedagogical implications, particularly in relation to the teaching of grammar. My own contribution examines translation as a test of the ability to write in a foreign language, on the basis of a restricted sample of examination scripts.

Machine translation is the most recent addition to the very long history of translation, and probably the most controversial. Viggo Hjørnager Pedersen and Helene Bekker-Nielsen Dunbar (Copenhagen University) discuss what one particular Computer Aided Translation programme, Winger 92, can offer the professional translator, going into both the advantages and the disadvantages of this use of technology.

Translation in all its shapes and forms is widely discussed and frequently criticised. It is my hope that this collection of articles will at the very least give readers something to think about.

A Mermaid Translated:

An analysis of some English versions of Hans Christian Andersen's 'Den lille Havfrue'

Viggo Hjørnager Pedersen

'The Little Mermaid' is one of Hans Christian Andersen's most popular stories, and exists in a great number of different English versions. The reason for its popularity is not far to seek. This very personal story, which is Andersen's original invention and not a traditional fairy- or folktale,[1] deals with very basic human concerns, social success and aspirations in love, certainly, but ultimately and fundamentally it treats of the deepest longings of the soul for harmony and self-realization. It does not really matter whether we view this in traditional Christian terms as did Andersen himself, or relate it to Jungian psychology like Eigil Nyborg (1983): in either case we are confronted with intense longing and endeavour which is defeated, the hope of redemption held out at the end being a not very welcome second best alternative, to the protagonist as well as to the author.

The essential elements of the story can be contained in a much shorter text than Andersen's, as proved by a number of successful English adaptations and abbreviations.[2] But the story is not just a kind of anti-fairy tale with an unhappy or resigned ending instead of the traditional happy one.[3] It is also one of Andersen's stylistic masterpieces, one in which Andersen's 'lyrical style' (Pedersen 1988:103) dominates almost throughout, a fact which is often very poorly reflected in English translations. There are, however, a number of fairly successful translations, and in the following I intend to look at the ways in which these seek to convey the stylistic and semantic nuances of Andersen's story.

I shall take Hersholt (1942-) as my point of departure, but his version will be compared with the earliest and still very readable version by Lady

The Dolphin 18
©Aarhus University Press 1990

Lucie Duff Gordon (1846) and with two other respectable modern versions, those of Eva le Gallienne (1971) and Poul Borum (1984).

In addition, H.W. Dulcken's version (undated) has been consulted, since Hersholt frequently uses Dulcken's texts as a basis for his own work. Although this does not seem to have been the case in the present instance,[4] Dulcken's pedestrian, but reasonably close, translation may sometimes serve as a useful foil when discussing more artistic translations.

Nothing is known about Duff Gordon's command of Danish; she is primarily known as a translator from the German, and may very well have used German versions as a support. Poul Borum is a contemporary Danish writer and critic. Jean Hersholt and Eva le Gallienne are both bilingual - Hersholt Danish by birth, le Gallienne English, with a Danish mother. Both produced their translations after they had taken up residence in the USA.

The approach employed in the following analysis is my own - cf. Pedersen (1988:110-111). Using concepts from the British linguistic tradition, it discusses translation problems at different levels or ranks: paragraph, sentence, phrase, and word, and recognizes five different operations: compression, deletion, addition, expansion, and change.

Paragraphs

Andersen has several relatively long paragraphs, most of them concerned with a description of the feelings of the protagonist or of the changing land- and seascape of the story. Hersholt breaks down many of these paragraphs, although he also removes some of Andersen's paragraph divisions. The absolute figures are 91 for Andersen and 102 for Hersholt, the latter figure being the result of 16 new paragraph divisions plus the removal of 5 of Andersen's.

Of the other translations, Borum here as in other respects follows Andersen, whereas le Gallienne adds 8 paragraph divisions, thus reaching a total of 99.

Andersen's paragraph divisions are certainly not always above reproach, and splitting up some of his longer paragraphs may in some respects be an advantage. Thus the fifth sister's adventure is described by Andersen in one paragraph, which Hersholt splits up into three, and at least the first of these new divisions (after '... lod Blæsten flyve med sit lange Haar' (A: 91.1))[5] seems reasonable enough (H: 61).

This applies even more when Andersen goes directly from the description of the Prince's birthday party to the shipwreck (A: 92.38). Here Hersholt's break (H: 63) after 'hun kunde see ind i Kahytten' appears quite justified.

8

On the other hand these changes do detract from Andersen's characteristic breathless rhythm.

Sentences

Here we find the same tendency as we found at paragraph level. Thus in Andersen's text the first two paragraphs are divided into five full stops (plus three semicolons) as against ten (plus one exclamation mark) in Hersholt (see Appendix 1). Whereas the change of paragraph structure is perhaps not of very great importance when the divergence is no greater than here, the corresponding shortening of periods does affect the style considerably. Andersen's prose is that of an exuberant *raconteur*, preserving many oral features in spite of the sentence length, which is often considerable:

> Matroserne dandsede paa Dækket, og da den unge Prinds traadte derud, steeg over hundrede Raketter op i Luften, de lyste, som den klare Dag, saa den lille Havfrue blev ganske forskrækket og dukkede ned under Vandet, men hun stak snart Hovedet igjen op, og da var det ligesom om alle Himmelens Stjerner faldt ned til hende. (A: 92.21-26)

Hersholt has no less than three full stops here, and thus completely changes the rhythm. His sentences are much less breathless than Andersen's, and may well be easier for untrained readers to cope with; but they are certainly very different from the original:

> Up on the deck the sailors were dancing, and when the Prince appeared among them a hundred or more rockets flew through the air, making it as bright as day. These startled the little mermaid so badly that she ducked under the water. But she soon peeped up again, and then it seemed as if all the stars in the sky were falling around her. (H: 63)

(See also the first two paragraphs in Appendix 1).

Formally the difference is reflected in the *syntactic structures* of the two texts: the first two paragraphs consist of a total of 5 periods comprising 18 clauses, 11 of which are main clauses, but in the third period nevertheless we reach the third and in the fifth the second degree of subordination. Hersholt has more periods (11), a total of 22 clauses with 14 main clauses, and only on one occasion do we get beyond the first degree of subordination.[6]

Later Danish editions of Andersen tend to modify the syntax of the first edition, and this may very well have influenced Hersholt. Nevertheless his version is certainly closer to the written norm than is Andersen's to that of the standard literary prose of his time.

A notable change when comparing the English syntax to the Danish is the loss of Danish inversion as in:

> Deilige grønne Høie med Viinranker saae hun (A: 90.12)
> She saw gloriously green, vine-colored hills (H: 60)
>
> deilige Stemmer havde de, smukkere, end noget Menneske (A: 91.15-16)
> They had beautiful voices, more charming than those of any mortal beings. (H: 62)
>
> hoppe og springe ville vi i de trehundrede Aar, vi have at leve i (A: 97.3-4)
> Let us leap and bound throughout the three hundred years that we have to live.
> (H: 68)

Quite apart from the fact that the rhythm changes, the Danish inversion lends an emphasis which goes well with the general tendency of the text towards colloquial hyperbole, and which is often lost in translation. Normally the only way of rendering it would be by introducing some sort of compensation such as an adverbial (e.g. 'She saw *the most* beautiful green hills'), unless one were to resort to cleft sentences as in Irish English ('It was lovely green hills with vines that she saw'). A more elegant version of the first solution is actually adopted in one case by le Gallienne, who renders the second example above as follows:

> They all had lovely voices, *far more* beautiful than any human voice, ... (L: 11)

The emphasis bestowed by the Danish word order has been moved to an adverb in the English apposition; but the important thing is that the emphasis has been kept.

Inversion, discussed by Jensen (1929:68-76), is a favourite device of Andersen's, used copiously right from his literary debut in *Fodreisen*:

> De Gamle maa Du studere ... Et nyt og bedre Menneske vil jeg gjøre Dig til.
> (Andersen 1986:10)

Consequently, Borum is right to emphasize the importance of this feature:

> Andersen's syntax is expressive and should not be betrayed. ... The most characteristic syntactical feature is the frontal position of the most important elements of the sentence. This is generally more common in the Scandinavian languages than in English, but Andersen's excessive use of it must be indicated. (B: 51)

However, one cannot approve of the way he tries to solve the problem in such examples as:

> lovely voices they had, more beautiful than any human being, ... (B: 32)

- which, apart from leading the reader to believe that 'voices' are being compared to 'human being', is barely acceptable in a modern text.

Another characteristic feature of Andersen's style is his use of main clauses in an asyndetic arrangement within the individual period as in the example from 92.21 quoted above - see Jensen (1929:214 ff). This may make the syntax look more hypotactic than it actually is; but when you read the text aloud it does make for speed.

Some examples can be found in the Appendices; the point to be noted here is that this feature is hardly ever preserved in English, such constructions being replaced either by subordination or a full stop - unless the compromise solution of semicolon or the introduction of a conjunction is resorted to:

> i hver ligge straalende Perler, een eneste vilde være stor Stads ... (A: Appendix 1)
> every shell holds glistening pearls, any one of which would be ... (H)

> den lille Havfrue følte ikke til Døden, hun saae den klare Sol (A: Appendix 2)
> the little mermaid did not feel the hand of death. In the bright sunlight overhead, she saw ...(H)
> the mermaid scarce felt the pains of death. She saw ... (D)

> Den lille Havfrue saae, at hun havde et Legeme som de, det hævede sig meer og meer ... (A: Appendix 2)
> The little mermaid discovered that she was shaped like them, and that she was gradually rising ... (H)

> men det er meget dybt, dybere end noget Ankertoug naaer (A: 87.3-4)
> but it is very deep; no anchor chain is long enough to fathom it (L:1)

Phrases and Collocations

It is at this level that the clumsy translator most easily reveals himself (see Pedersen 1988:132 ff), and even respectable translations often fall short. In the present instance, the very first line of the story signals that something is slightly wrong. 'Far out in the ocean' (H: 57) is as unnatural an opening for an English text as 'Langt ude i Havet' is natural for a Danish one - cf. 'Der var so dejligt ude på landet', the celebrated opening of Andersen's

'Ugly Duckling'. Adverb of place + defining prepositional complement is odd in English - normally the prepositional phrase would suffice: 'It was lovely in the country' rather than '... out in the country', as one frequently finds in translations of this tale.

However, there are fewer problems involving set phrases and standard collocations in 'The Little Mermaid' than are normally encountered in Andersen - presumably because the style is lyrical throughout, with relatively little dialogue and a limited use of humorous colloquialisms.

Some examples of problem areas:

Tautologies (taken in the loose sense of two more or less synonymous words used where one would presumably do) are easy enough to render, if one takes the trouble. However, finding proper equivalents for both members of a tautology may be difficult; thus in the present story, 'Slotte og Gaarde' (A: 90.13) for some reason seems to be a problem: 'Palaces and manor houses' (H: 60), 'Palaces and castles' (Du: 475) 'castles and houses' (D: 38) - where Hersholt and Dulcken exaggerate and Duff Gordon misses the agricultural implications of 'Gaarde'.

'Hoppe og springe' (A: 97.3-4) - by Borum with ludicrous effect rendered as 'hop and skip' (B: 38) is really not much better in Hersholt's version: 'leap and bound' (H: 68). The best solution is decidedly 'dance and sing and be merry' (D: 47), which is exactly what the Danish means, even if it is not quite an idiom.

Hersholt sometimes introduces this construction with good effect: 'Crawl and sprawl about on her spongy bosom' (H: 70) = 'vælte sig på hendes store, svampede Bryst' (A: 98.31-32); 'crawl and sprawl' seems much better than 'crawl about' (L: 29) or 'tumble around' (B: 39), and it recreates a typical feature of Andersen's style, which must be given up in other places.

Idioms, as mentioned, are few. The one that immediately springs to mind is 'man maae lide noget for Stadsen' (A: 92.1), the terse under-statement of which seems to be difficult to render:[7]

> You must put up with a good deal to keep up appearances, (H: 62)
> Young ladies must not mind trifling inconveniences ... when they dress to go out (D: 40)
> pride must suffer pain (Du: 477)

Hersholt's translation is quite inadequate, Duff Gordon's here as in other places exhibits a tendency to overtranslate - she attempts to relocate Andersen's fairyland to polite British nineteenth century society (cf. her translation of 'Ingen var saa længselsfuld som den yngste' (A: 89.14) as 'But of all the sisters, not one longed for her release from the restraints of childhood so ardently as the youngest' (D: 37)). Dulcken, for once, seems to have the best solution, retaining the terseness of the original, although failing to preserve the faintly derogatory associations of 'stads'.[8]

'Reenlighed er en god Ting' (A: 100.4-5), which alludes to a Danish proverb ('Renlighed er en god ting, sagde kællingen, hun vendte sin særk nytårsaften'), is rendered by Hersholt somewhat unimaginatively as 'Cleanliness is a good thing' (H: 71), whereas Duff Gordon introduces a corresponding proverb: 'Cleanliness is next to Godliness' (D: 51); Borum here, as in other places, is inadequate from an artistic point of view, however close his translation may be: 'Cleanliness is always good' (B: 41).

Words

We are not here concerned with random changes like le Gallienne's 'vineyards' (L: 8) for 'Viinranker' (A: 90.12) which do not really matter, because the clauses into which they enter are reasonably equivalent: 'Deilige grønne Høie med Viinranker saae hun' = 'She saw beautiful green hills covered with vineyards'. What we are concerned with are problems of rendering adequately words that constitute Andersen's world (frequently specifically Danish terms) or which are characteristic of his style.

'The Little Mermaid' is set in a nondescript fairyland, which is characterized in very general terms. Hence there are no problems with nouns without any equivalent in English, as is often the case when Andersen is concerned with specifically Danish milieus, as in 'Nissen hos Spekhøkeren' (see Pedersen, 1988:99 ff).

Some adjectives, on the other hand, are quite tricky. This goes for the numerous compounds, particularly some designating colour, and for a number of descriptive adjectives that mainly convey some sort of vague romantic feeling, the catchwords, one might say, of the Nordic twilight of Oehlenschläger and his followers. Below, a couple of examples will be discussed.

Forunderlig: 'et forunderligt blaat Skjær' (A: 88.13) (cf. 'de forunderligste Skikkelser' (A: 90.38) and 'et forunderligt dybt Suk' (A: 105.20-21)). The word has a Biblical ring to it ('Store og forunderlige ere dine Gierninger, Herre') - cf. Pre-Romantic and Romantic uses of the word as in 'Forunderligt at sige, og sært at tænke på' (Brorson). This is a real Hans Christian Andersen word, conveying not only strangeness, but wonder. Hence 'wondrous' (D: 36) is a good solution to render A: 88.13, whereas 'peculiar' (Du: 473) is not: quite apart from the modern associations of 'funny peculiar', the word fails to render the connotations of the original.

Længselsfuld, too, is a loaded word. 'O kom du hulde, sig hvi kan du tøve / at synke til mit længselsfulde Bryst' exclaims the Romantic poet Staffeldt (*Ordbog over det danske Sprog*, 1975). The Romantic poets, celebrating the unattainable, used the word copiously, and Andersen followed suit:

> Ingen var saa længelsfuld som den yngste (A. 89.14)
> The most eager of them all was the youngest (H: 59)
> But of all the sisters, not one longed for her release from the restraints of childhood so ardently as the youngest (D: 37)
> No one was more anxious about these things than the youngest (Du: 474)
> Not one of them was as impatient as the youngest princess (L: 6)

None of these translations really catch the tone of the Danish. 'Eager' and 'impatient' are too energetic and self-reliant, 'longed for' is too weak, and when this is compensated for by the addition of the adverbial phrase 'so ardently', the result becomes too ponderous; and as for 'anxious', it introduces a note of fear which is not present in the original.

'Længsel' is 'yearning', hence the adjective here might perhaps be rendered by a verbal paraphrase with 'yearn for'; only this would, of course, necessitate the introduction of an object. However, a possible solution might be a fairly close translation: 'None was so full of yearning as the youngest'.

Forskrækkelig is a different case. Originally it simply meant 'frightening', but at Andersen's time it had come to be employed very often with reduced meaning, like English 'awful': 'det var hende næsten det forskrækkeligste' (A: 98.23) may still be close to the original meaning; but when in 'The Princess and the Pea' we learn that the situation 'var ganske forskrækkelig', we have the reduced sense. At all events, 'a ghastly sight' (H: 70) is perhaps slightly exaggerated as the translation of A: 98.23, whereas 'you may guess how frightened the poor princess was at sight of this' (D: 49) goes to the other extreme.

Sometimes things that might be considered offensive are left out in otherwise full translations like those under discussion. This, too, often applies to adjectives, though other parts of speech may of course also be affected:

> vælte sig paa hendes store, svampede Bryst (A: 98.31-32)
> lie on her lap (D: 49)

> de nydeligste smaae, hvide Been (A: 100.37-38)
> the most beautiful legs (D:52)

Compound Adjectives are not well tolerated by the English language, so most of Andersen's must be reduced or analysed into their component parts:

    det allerklareste Rav (A: 87.14)
    the clearest amber (H: 57)

    den stjerneblaae Himmel (A: 104.37)
    the star fields of the blue sky (H: 76)

    det dødskolde havskum (A: 105.35)
    the chill sea foam (H: 77)
    the waves (D: 59)
    the deathly chill of the sea foam (L: 46)

Comparison of the Three Versions

An analysis like the above is only the raw material for a comparative appraisal of a group of translations such as those discussed here. It is also necessary to look at the various characteristic features of the translations in combination in order to assess their compound effect.

If, therefore, we turn to the examples in Appendix 2, it is evident that none of these quite follow Andersen's syntax, though Borum comes very close - so close, in fact, that the style of his translation suffers (thus 'mildly' and 'warmly' in line 2 are used exactly as in Danish, but they are unidiomatic in the English sentence).

Hersholt's translation is good and quite close to Andersen, the main but important difference being the change of syntax already commented on.

Both the other translations are freer than Borum's and Hersholt's.

Duff Gordon has the advantage of being closest to Andersen in time, so that her formulations often strike us as natural nineteenth century equivalents for Andersen's. She, too, tends to normalize syntax, however, and she often leaves out details that are difficult or which she regards as unimportant or too emphatic. Thus instead of 'dødskolde Havskum' (Appendix 2) she has simply 'waves', which is typical of her tendency to simplify by means of compression, cf.

    deilige grønne Høie (A: 90.12)
    green hills (D: 38)

    hun var ganske nøgen (A: 100.39)
    she was naked (D: 52)

Eva le Gallienne's version, on the other hand, is a fine modern translation. She does not modify Andersen's syntax as much as does Hersholt, but she does take those little liberties that are necessary in order to recreate a literary text in another language; thus in the paragraph quoted in Appendix 2 she introduces the connecting phrase 'So transparent were they, that...', and 'svævede ved deres egen Lethed' is rendered adequately and simply by 'floated like gossamer'.

Conclusion

In conclusion I should like to emphasize that even though I prefer Eva le Gallienne's version, all the translations discussed here are reasonably good; any of them should enable English-speaking audiences to obtain a fair impression of Andersen. Moreover, the effect of this story depends to a large extent on the imagery, which comes across in any full translation.

Danish readers may still feel that something of Andersen's magic is missing and want to exclaim, 'Bless thee, mermaid, thou art translated!' But translation is the price that must be paid for bringing Andersen's art to a wider audience, as he himself so heartily desired; and even if the translations may look a little like a mermaid out of water, Andersen himself when sending his creation abroad would no doubt have told her, 'thou losest here, a better where to find'.

Appendix 1

Langt ude i Havet er Vandet saa blaat, som Bladene paa den deiligste Kornblomst og saa klart, som det reneste Glas, men det er meget dybt, dybere end noget Ankertoug naaer, mange Kirketaarne maatte stilles ovenpaa hinanden, for at række fra Bunden op over Vandet. Dernede boe Havfolkene.

Nu maa man slet ikke troe, at der kun er den nøgne hvide Sandbund; nei, der voxe de forunderligste Træer og Planter, som ere saa smidige i Stilk og Blade, at de ved den mindste Bevægelse af Vandet røre sig, ligesom om de vare levende. Alle Fiskene, smaae og store, smuttede imellem Grenene, ligesom heroppe Fuglene i Luften. Paa det allerdybeste Sted ligger Havkongens Slot, Murene ere af Coraller og de lange spidse Vinduer af det allerklareste Rav, men Taget er Muslingskaller, der aabne og lukke sig, eftersom Vandet gaaer; det seer deiligt ud; thi i hver ligge straalende Perler, een eneste vilde være stor Stads i en Dronnings Krone. (A: 87)

Far out in the ocean the water is as blue as the petals of the loveliest cornflower, and as clear as the purest glass. But it is very deep too. It goes down deeper than any anchor rope will go, and many, many steeples would have to be stacked one on top of another to reach from the bottom to the surface of the sea. It is down there that the sea folk live.

Now don't suppose that there are only bare white sands at the bottom of the sea. No indeed! The most marvellous trees and flowers grow down there, with such pliant stalks and leaves that the least stir in the water makes them move about as though they were alive. All sorts of fish, large and small, dart among the branches, just as birds flit through the trees up here. From the deepest spot in the ocean rises the palace of the sea king. Its walls are made of coral and its high pointed windows of the clearest amber, but the roof is made of mussel shells that open and shut with the tide. This is a wonderful sight to see, for every shell holds glistening pearls, any one of which would be the pride of a queen's crown. (H: 57)

Appendix 2

Nu steeg Solen frem af Havet. Straalerne faldt saa mildt og varmt paa det dødskolde Havskum og den lille Havfrue følte ikke til Døden, hun saae den klare Sol, og oppe over hende svævede hundrede gjennemsigtige, deilige Skabninger; hun kunde gjennem dem see Skibets hvide Seil og Himlens røde Skyer, deres Stemme var Melodie, men saa aandig, at intet menneskeligt Øre kunde høre den, ligesom intet jordisk Øie kunne see dem; uden Vinger svævede de ved deres egen Lethed gjennem Luften. Den lille Havfrue saae, at hun havde et Legeme som de, det hævede sig meer og meer op af Skummet. (A: 105-106)

The sun rose up from the waters. Its beams fell, warm and kindly, upon the chill sea foam, and the little mermaid did not feel the hand of death. In the bright sunlight overhead, she saw hundreds of fair ethereal beings. They were so transparent that through them she could see the ship's white sails and the red clouds in the sky. Their voices were sheer music, but so spirit-like that no human ear could detect the sound, just as no eye on earth could see their forms. Without wings, they floated as light as the air itself.

The little mermaid discovered that she was shaped like them, and that she was gradually rising up out of the foam. (H: 77-78)

And now the sun rose out of the sea, and its rays fell so warm and bright upon the waves, that the mermaid scarce felt the pains of death. She saw the red sun and the white sails of the ship, and the rose-coloured clouds, and, floating in the air above her, thousands of lovely transparent creatures, whose heavenly voices could not be heard any more than their airy shapes can be seen by men. They had no wings, but floated along, lighter than the air which bore them. And the mermaid now saw that her body had become like theirs, and that she was rising out of the foam into the air. (D: 59)

The sun rose above the horizon; its mild rays warmed the deathly chill of the sea foam so that the little mermaid didn't feel the pangs of death. She saw the bright sun, and then she saw, floating above her, hundreds of the most exquisite translucent creatures; so transparent were they, that she could see the white sails of the ship and the rosy clouds in the sky right through them. Their voices were like music, but so ethereal that no human ear could hear them, just as no human eye could ever see their forms. They had no wings, but they were so light they floated on the air like gossamer.

The little mermaid started to assume a shape like theirs, and gradually felt herself emerging from the sea foam. (L: 46-48)

Now the sun rose out of the sea, the rays fell so mildly and warmly on the death-cold[9] sea foam, and the little mermaid did not feel death, she saw the clear sun, and up there a hundred lovely, transparent shapes were floating; straight through them she could see the white sails of the ship and the red clouds of the sky, their voices were a melody, but so ethereal that no earthly ear could hear it, just as no earthly eye could see them; without wings they floated by their own lightness through the air. The little mermaid saw that she had a body like theirs, it rose out of the foam more and more. (B: 46)

Notes

1. Almost every study of Andersen's tales discusses 'The Little Mermaid', its origins, its place in Andersen's *oeuvre*, or its relation to the folk tradition. The origins are discussed by Brix (1970:77-81) and Kofoed (1967:189 ff). A fascinating psychological (Jungian) study is found in Nyborg (1983), and an attempt at a refutation of Nyborg's thesis that the story is about Andersen's subconscious realization of the fact that his individuation process was never completed is found in Baggesen (1967). The two latter analyses are of interest for translation studies because the religious element, and particularly the concluding paragraphs about the daughters of the air are often left out in English versions for children. Apparently a number of translators and editors intuitively tend to agree with Nyborg's contention that the Christian element is not central to the meaning of the story.
2. I am here referring to versions like those described in Note 1, or to even more radical reinterpretations in which the prince marries the mermaid, thus bringing the story closer to the traditional fairytale (cf. Pedersen, forthcoming, about similar tendencies in English versions of 'The Ugly Duckling'). But there are many examples of successful versions which simply shorten the tale, usually by leaving

out some of the exploits of the other mermaids and some details in the descriptions of the worlds above and under the water, without essentially changing the message of the tale. This applies to the adaption by Anathea Bell (Andersen 1984b) and to the anonymous Andersen (undated).

3. Bettelheim (1975) points out that a fairy-tale must have a happy ending because in symbolic form it deals with the problems of maturation and is designed to help young people to come to terms with their subconscious conflicts and fears.

4. In attempting to establish the dependence of a translation on an earlier one, the obvious procedure is to look for similarities of formulation, particularly in the case of oblique or wrong translations of detail not found in other texts. Such an investigation shows that Hersholt does not follow Dulcken; but he must be influenced by Duff Gordon. Like her he translates 'den dybeste Sø' (A: 88.1 Note 5) by 'the deep sea' (H: 57) rather than by the correct 'the deepest lake' (B: 29). It is true that this feature is also found in other English translations. But there are other examples, one of the most significant being 'white arms' (D: 37, H: 59) for 'hvide hænder' (A: 89.24), instead of 'white hands' (Du: 474).

5. In the following, A = Andersen, B = Borum, D = Duff Gordon, Du = Dulcken, H = Hersholt, and L = le Gallienne.

6. The exclamation 'No indeed!' has been counted as a period. Otherwise, only finite constructions have been counted as clauses.

7. 'Stads', derived from Medieval Latin 'statio' and cognate with 'station', was associated with the pomp of religious processions, hence with pomp in general. Negative associations developed later, and at Andersen's time were well established: 'Hvad giør det, om der er en Autor mere eller mindre i Verden, det Stads løber i Veiret, saa det er istand til at æde os op' (ODS - Andersen). Andersen uses the term in both negative and positive senses; and in an example like 'stor stads' the negative associations, though not uppermost in a native speaker's mind, are nevertheless present.

8. The reason is not far to seek: Dulcken has taken over this phrase from Madame de Chatelain, a good translator of Andersen, whose *Tales and Fairy Stories* first appeared in 1852.

9. The original divides the word over two lines, so it is impossible to see whether Borum means 'deathcold' or 'death-cold'.

Bibliography

Andersen, H.C. (1963-) Den lille Havfrue. Dal, E. and Nielsen, E. (eds.) *H.C. Andersens Eventyr* I: 87-111. Copenhagen.

Andersen, H.C. (undated) *The Little Mermaid* (Hans Andersen Museum number 1042/1980). London.

Andersen, H.C. (undated) *The Little Mermaid* (transl. by H.W. Dulcken - British Library catalogue number 12809/k10) Ca. 1870). London.

Andersen, H.C. (1949) The Little Mermaid (transl. by Jean Hersholt - 1st ed. 1942-). *The Complete Andersen*, vol. 5. New York.

Andersen, H.C. (1971) *The Little Mermaid* (transl. by Eva le Gallienne). New York.

Andersen, H.C. (1972) The Little Mermaid (transl. by Lucie Duff Gordon). *The Little Mermaid and her Story*. (Ed. Grønlund publishers). Copenhagen.

Andersen, H.C. (1984a) *The Little Mermaid* (transl. by Poul Borum). Holstebro.

Andersen, H.C. (1984b) *The Little Mermaid* (adapted by Anathea Bell). London.

Andersen, H.C. (1986) *En Fodreise fra Holmens Canal til Østpynten af Amager i Aarene 1828 og 1829* (1829) ed. J. de Mylius. Copenhagen.

Baggesen, S. (1967) 'Individuation eller frelse' *Kritik I*: 50-77. Copenhagen.

Bettelheim, B. (1975) *The Uses of Enchantment*. London.

Bredsdorff, E. (1954) *H.C. Andersen og England*. Copenhagen.

Brix, H. (1970) *H.C. Andersen og hans Eventyr*. (1st ed. 1907). Copenhagen.

Jensen, Anker (1929) *Studier over H.C. Andersens Sprog*. Haderslev.

Kofoed, N. (1967) *H.C. Andersens fortællekunst*. Copenhagen.

Ordbog over det danske Sprog (ODS) (1975 - 1st ed. 1919 ff). Copenhagen.

Pedersen, V.H. (forthcoming) 'Ugly Ducklings? Reflections on some English Versions of Hans Andersen's "Den grimme Ælling"'. To be published in *Proceedings of SSOTT III*. Oslo.

Pedersen, V.H. (1988) *Essays on Translation*. Copenhagen.

Nyborg, Eigil (1983) *Den indre linie i H.C. Andersens eventyr*. (2nd ed. - 1st ed. 1962). Copenhagen.

Words, Words, Words

Hanne Tang Grödal

Some hold translations not unlike to be
The wrong side of a Turkey tapestry.

James Howell

Little did I think when I first attended Shirley Larsen's courses in translation some eighteen years ago that I would actually end up translating almost every day, let alone make a living out of it. In spite of my teacher's efforts to make the classes interesting and varied it was not a favourite discipline of mine, I did not relish looking up endless words in various dictionaries, and I was not particularly good at it either. Many years later I suddenly and unexpectedly found myself - it was not my own idea - translating a book about a young woman who had crossed the Australian desert with four camels. I must confess that for quite a while I felt rather like a pathless wanderer in the desert myself with not even a camel to lean on. My first chapter came back with an alarming number of corrections - it is customary to let beginners translate a trial chapter, and all the corrections were excellent and very precise, I might add - and I thought, this is never going to work. Some of the teaching from my early university days must have stuck, however, for I did finish the book although I found it a very slow and painstaking process. But there was also an element of fascination which led me on and became a driving force through all the nitty-gritty details of the translation work that was to follow. This fascination was and is for me twofold: the immersion in a literary text, the complete involvement in a fictional universe which takes on a different quality when one focuses so closely on the language, and at the same time cool observation, the challenging and thrilling knowledge that somehow this text is to be rendered into Danish. This combination of closeness and distance is of course present in any analysis of a literary text, but when I compared it with teaching literature I found that I gained an insight on another level, not necessarily thematically or analytically, rather something that concerned the craftsmanship of the writer; perhaps one could call it getting a glimpse of the writer's workshop. In the beginning I became so caught up in details that I tended to lose the general view. But like so many other things in this profession, that is a matter of routine.

> What do you read, my Lord?
> Words, words, words.
>
> *Hamlet*, Act II

And how to string all those words together, there's the rub.

> First I do a draft translation, an extremely rough draft translation; an outline. After that I go through the text in detail and fill in more and more. It is a laborious process, repeated several times, extremely hard work. The text becomes like a sculpture, a sculpture made of a million elements which I put in, pull out and fiddle with. But the sculpture image does not go far enough: the text has more than three dimensions. The language moves all the time. (Kerstin Gustafsson; my translation).[1]

The Swedish translator quoted here touches on an essential element in the approach to a text in the translation process, the organic quality of the language and the *life* of the text itself. A colleague expresses it in another way: be open to the text, let it come to you and do not read anything into it that is not there.[2] First of all, I think it is important that you like the text you are going to translate. When I read it through the first time, I usually underline the difficult parts, write down suggestions and make a sort of brief analysis, determining the style and tone and rhythm. These last three elements are just as important as looking up the right words in the dictionary, for they 'decide' in a way whether the finished translation works at all. Sometimes I start in the middle and then go back to the beginning in order to ensure an even fluency all the way through, but it depends on the text. In contrast to the Swedish translator quoted above, I normally attempt to come close to the finished polished product from the very start, although I have taught myself to leave the more difficult problems and return to them in the next round. It saves time and as a rule I am more apt to come up with inspired solutions, when there are only a few 'holes' left in the text. Then I read the finished product, comparing it with the source language text, and I know translators who recommend that it be put aside for two weeks and then finally reread on its own.[3] From whichever angle it suits one's temperament to approach this process, it is always a matter of *choice*; one chooses what one finds to be the right words, often among a number of synonyms. So it is of course a rendering of the original text, but it is also a particular interpretation of it.

> He is Translation's thief that addeth more
> As much as he that taketh from the store
> of the first author.
>
> Andrew Marwell

In the contract that you sign with a publisher before you start translating, for instance, a novel, you undertake to deliver a faithful translation of the original. The question is of course how far you can go in your own interpretation before you stray away from the original. As a general rule I keep close to the text, but in the end it is the text itself that determines my approach, the writer's syntax and style and craftsmanship. Two widely different American writers, Louise Erdrich and Marge Piercy, illustrate my point, and I have translated two novels by each. Louise Erdrich belongs to a younger group of writers; she is very conscious of what she is doing, how she is using the language, she is economical in her writing and very precise:

'Ante a dollar then,' said Fleur, and pitched hers in. She lost, but they let her scrape along, a cent at a time. And then she won some. She played unevenly, as if chance were all she had. She reeled them in. The game went on. The dog was stiff now, poised on Lily's knees, a ball of vicious muscle with its yellow eyes slit in concentration. It gave advice, seemed to sniff the lay of Fleur's cards, twitched and nudged. Fleur was up, then down, saved by a scratch. Tor dealt seven cards, three down. The pot grew, round by round, until it held all the money. Nobody folded. Then it rode on one last card and they went silent. Fleur picked hers up and drew a long breath. The heat lowered like a bell. Her card shook, but she stayed in.[4]

'Så en dollar op,' sagde Fleur og smed sin ind. Hun tabte, men de lod hende hutle sig igennem med en cent ad gangen. Og så vandt hun lidt. Hun spillede ujævnt, som om heldet var det eneste, hun havde. Hun halede dem ind. Spillet fortsatte. Nu var hunden stiv, som den balancerede på Lilys knæ, en bylt af arrige muskler og de gule øjensprækker smalle af koncentration. Den gav gode råd, syntes at kunne snuse sammensætningen af Fleurs kort, rykkede og puffede. Fleur var oppe, så nede, blev reddet på et hængende hår. Tor gav syv kort, tre ned. Puljen voksede, omgang efter omgang indtil den rummede alle pengene. Ingen lagde kortene. Så beroede det hele på det sidste kort, og de blev tavse. Fleur trak sit og tog en dyb indånding. Heden lagde sig som en klokke. Hendes kort rystede, men hun blev i spillet. (My translation).

Her language is intense, and at times her prose moves into poetry:

> Our mothers warn us that we'll think he's handsome, for he appears with green eyes, copper skin, a mouth tender as a child's. But if you fall into his arms, he sprouts horns, fangs, claws, fins. His feet are joined as one and his skin, brass scales, rings to the touch. You're fascinated, cannot move. He casts a shell necklace at your feet, weeps gleaming chips that harden into mica on your breasts. He holds you under. Then he takes the body of a lion, a fat brown worm, or a familiar man. He's made of gold. He's made of beach moss. He's a thing of dry foam, a thing of death by drowning, the death a Chippewa cannot survive.[5]

> Vores mødre advarer os mod, at vi skal synes han er flot, for han viser sig med grønne øjne, kobbergylden hud, en mund så blid som et barns. Men hvis man falder i hans arme, skyder der horn, hugtænder, kløer og finner frem. Hans ben hænger sammen, og hans hud af messingskæl ringer, når man rører ved den. Man er tryllebundet, kan ikke bevæge sig. Han kaster en halskæde af muslingeskaller for fødderne af en, græder skinnende spåner, der stivner til marieglas på ens bryster. Han holder en under vandet. Så tager han skikkelse af en løve, en tyk brun orm eller en velkendt mand. Han er af guld. Han er af strandmos. Han er en skabning af tørt skum, en druknedødens skabning, en død en chippewa ikke kan overleve. (My translation).

Marge Piercy, on the other hand, tends to construct her sentences in a looser fashion, she overflows where the other is concise:

> In Washington she had had to share a tiny room at the Mayflower that would obviously until this year have been a smallish single with Dorothy McMichaels, who under an array of pseudonyms spewed out two to four stories a month for the confession magazines. Dorothy was conservative, religious, a true believer in sexual sin and retribution, a loose-limbed, loud-voiced woman who made Louise remember social workers she had known when she was an orphan being placed in foster homes in Cleveland.[6]

> På Hotel Mayflower i Washington havde hun måttet dele et lille bitte værelse, som indtil i år tydeligvis havde været et mindre enkeltværelse, med Dorothy McMichaels der under et hav af pseudonymer udspyede mellem to og fire historier om måneden til romanbladene. Dorothy var konservativ og religiøs, en ranglet, højrøstet kvinde som troede fuldt og fast på at sex var syndigt og burde straffes, og som fik Louise til at tænke på de socialrådgivere hun havde kendt, da hun blev forældreløs og skulle anbringes hos en plejefamilie i Cleveland. (My translation).

With Erdrich I stick very close to the text, every single nuance is important, and one gets the impression that every single word has been chosen with care. With Piercy I often feel the necessity of stepping back, after having dived into the text as it were, stepping back and constructing the sentences 'at a distance'. Then there are the syntactical differences between the languages, for instance, the tendency in English to use a noun whereas in Danish we prefer a verb phrase. Every novel usually has its own culture-specific terminology, problems that can sometimes be difficult to solve if we do not have a corresponding phenomenon or expression in Danish, but in general it is a good idea to keep in mind that the fictional universe one is translating *is* foreign, and that this 'foreignness' should not be glossed over. The result is often long searches in reference works and encyclopedias and consultations with research librarians, friends or relatives who happen to be experts within a specific field. The Piercy novel quoted above is about the Second World War, which involved a considerable amount of research concerning bombs, airplanes, intelligence agencies etc., because the writer had obviously made an effort to be historically correct. Recently I worked on a novel that contained a number of slang expressions and modern jargon. I consulted dictionaries of slang but also talked to my teenage daughter, who brought me up to date on some of the latest expressions in 'hip jargon'. So although translating is a fairly lonely job, the world of books does necessitate contact, not only with other books but also with other worlds outside the books. Knowledge of different cultures, lifestyles etc. is in a way also required, and acquired along the way. Contacting the novelists themselves is also an experience which can be both helpful and interesting.

> My old friend, Mrs. Carter, could make a
> pudding as well as translate Epictetus.
>
> Samuel Johnson

Translators keep the language alive, they reflect on the wide range of choices and possibilities.[7] They do in other words have a role to play within cultural communication. But it is not a very visible role, although things are improving, and translation still needs to be taken seriously on its own terms as a craft and as a profession - not least financially. And it still needs to be reviewed properly, for often a translation is not even mentioned,[8] and when it is, it is rarely judged as a whole, blunders and anglicisms being singled out instead. In spite of that I still find it fascinating, more and more so in fact, to delve into books in the English language, hopefully to combine the nitty-gritty with some linguistic creativeness and to recreate the worlds in and behind the words.

Notes

1. Det första jag gör är en råöversätning, en oerhört grov råöversätning; en skiss. Sedan går jag varv efter varv och fyller i mer och mer. Det är arbetsamma genomgångar, ett knådande utan like. Texten blir som en skulptur, en skulptur av miljoner material, som jag trycker in, drar ut och pusslar med. Men skulpturassociationen räcker inte: texten har många fler dimensioner än tre. Språket rör sig hela tiden. Kerstin Gustafsson i *Översättaran*, no. 7, 1988, p.3.
2. Lisbeth Møller-Madsen, personal communication.
3. Lisbeth Møller-Madsen, personal communication.
4. Louise Erdrich: *Tracks*, Henry Holt & Co., New York, 1988, p.23. Danish version: *Spor*, Gyldendal, 1989, p.28.
5. Ibid. p.11, Danish version p.18.
6. Marge Piercy: *Gone to Soldiers*, Michael Joseph, London, 1987, p.94. Danish version: *I krig*, Gyldendal 1989, p.128.
7. Johannes Riis in a talk at a workshop on translation in Forfatterforeningen, June 1988.
8. Niels Brunse in *Forfatteren*, February 1986/1.

Problems of Inconformity:
Some Danish Word Types and their English Equivalents

Knud Sørensen

A rough comparison between the structures of English and Danish appears to lead to the conclusion that there are a great many similarities between the two languages. For instance the generalization may be formulated that there is a fairly high degree of word-class conformity between English and Danish: a translator will note that most English nouns translate naturally into Danish nouns, and that in the majority of cases adjectives correspond to adjectives, etc. Similarly, on the basis of typical equivalences like 'a surprising story': *en overraskende historie* and 'a flattering remark': *en smigrende bemærkning* one might be tempted to equate *-ing* in this function with *-ende*. Such equations are of course useful for translation purposes, and they are undoubtedly valid up to a point. But they clearly do not capture the whole truth. In the following pages we shall take a look at three areas where there turns out to be a mixture of conformity and inconformity between English and Danish; this will be done in the belief that a contrastive perspective is often helpful.

1. Danish Participles in *-ende* and their English Equivalents

It can hardly be doubted that on a statistical basis a dominant translation equivalence could be set up between Danish adjectival participles in *-ende* and English participles in *-ing*. Examples like the following are numerous:

en forstående holdning - 'an understanding attitude'
en spændende oplevelse - 'an exciting experience'
af blivende betydning - 'of lasting importance'

Of course it is sometimes possible to find cases where this equation does not apply, or applies only partially: 'ingratiating' corresponds to both *indsmigrende* and *slesk*, and besides, English has available the adjective 'ingratiatory'. Nevertheless, the *-ende/-ing* equivalence is the dominant one. In very many cases, then, both languages exploit the present participle to form adjectives. But there is not total conformity, and that is why this is a troublesome area for translators. In the first place the English *-ing* ending competes with the *-y* ending in a number of cases; in the second place *-ing* is sometimes non-existent in an adjectival function, being replaced by Romance endings like *-ant*, *-ent*, and *-ive*; and in the third place Danish forms in *-ende* sometimes correspond to English nouns.

1.1. Let us begin by considering the competition between *-ing* and *-y* adjectives. In some cases there is little or no difference between the two adjectival types, so that *dangling* and *dangly*, *drooping* and *droopy*, *flickering* and *flickery* are practically interchangeable, though there is a tendency for the *-y* forms to be felt as somewhat more colloquial than the *-ing* forms. Sometimes there is a tendency for an *-ing* adjective to be neutral while the corresponding *-y* adjective is emotional: 'a *preaching* friar' is an objective expression, while a derogatory note is conveyed by 'He seems smug and *preachy*'. The words 'a *dripping* tap' give factual information, while in 'a *drippy* love story' we have an emotional expression, *drippy* meaning 'sentimental'. Compare further 'a *sniffing* dog' and 'a *sniffy* (=arrogant) comment'.

In other cases there is the difference between the two types that *-ing* adjectives are semantically unmarked, *-y* adjectives marked. What this means is that *-ing* adjectives can refer to either a specific phenomenon of limited duration, for instance: *a blushing bride, a bouncing ball, a gurgling noise*, or to a permanent feature: *bulging eyes, a squeaking voice, a wandering scholar*, while *-y* adjectives have a narrower semantic range, being used to describe permanent or characteristic features: *a squeaky voice, a bouncy sofa, a rocky marriage*.

Sometimes there is partial overlap between the two types. Thus we speak of a *catching* disease and of a *catchy* tune, but gaiety can be described as being either *catching* or *catchy*. We speak of *running* water and of a *running* commentary, and of *runny* (semi-liquid) butter or jam; but a nose can be characterized by either adjective.

1.2. While the *-ing*/*-y* competition discussed above is found with derivatives of a number of verbs having an expressive phonetic structure (cf. examples like frequentative *flicker* and echoic *squeak*), the group of adjectives to be dealt with next are related to verbs of Romance origin. It is important to realize this fact if we are to understand why the adjective corresponding to *evade* is *evasive*. For the origin of 'evasive' is French *èvasif, -ive*, while the verb 'evade' is based on French *èvader*. It is true that the form *evading* also exists, but it occurs exclusively in a verbal function, as in 'she was evading my question', so that the normal way of forming a participial adjective by adding *-ing* to the verb does not apply in this and similar cases.

The dominant ending of such French-inspired adjectives is *-ive*, and it may be useful to give some additional examples of them, the corresponding Danish form in *-ende* being given in italics; it goes without saying that there are other possible translations of the adjectives, but an *-ende* form seems natural in these cases:

an attractive offer: *tiltrækkende*
creative imagination: *skabende*
an elusive reply: *undvigende*
extensive studies: *omfattende*
an impressive achievement: *imponerende*
an intrusive visitor: *påtrængende*
a provocative remark: *provokerende*
a repulsive appearance: *frastødende*
subversive activities: *(stats)undergravende*

Besides *provocative* there is also the form *provoking* (= annoying). Very occasionally both *-ing* and *-ive* occur: the *decisive* (or *deciding*) factor, a *dismissive* (or *dismissing*) gesture. These appear to be used indiscriminately, though the form in parenthesis is the less frequent one.

Other, less frequent, Romance endings are *-ant* and *-ent*:

a soft, hesitant voice: *tøvende*
a triumphant shout: *triumferende*
his repellent views: *frastødende*

Compare also an *apologetic* tone (*undskyldende*). It may be noted that the adjective *hesitant* usually indicates a general tendency to hesitate, while the form *hesitating* is used about individual situations.

To redress the balance it may be useful to repeat that in most cases it is possible to form participial adjectives in *-ing*, and that the *-ant*, *-ent*, and *-ive* adjectives form a minority, albeit an important one.

1.3. Danish participles in *-ende* appear in two functions:

a) as attributive adjectives: *de badende piger, de strejkende arbejdere*; in this function there is normally no translation problem (apart from the cases just discussed): *-ende* corresponds to *-ing*

b) employed substantively: *de(n) badende, de strejkende*; in this function there is often inconformity between the two languages, for where English has available an agent noun corresponding in sense to the Danish participle, that noun must be used. Thus the Danish examples just given correspond to English 'the bather(s)' and 'the striker(s)'. Similar cases are *de dansende*: 'the dancers'; *de ferierende*: 'the holiday makers'; *de lidende*: 'the sufferers'; *to overlevende*: 'two survivors'; *en rejsende*: 'a traveller'; *de sovende*: 'the sleepers'; *en troende*: 'a believer'; *de krigsførende*: 'the belligerents'.

This paragraph is not strictly speaking relevant in a discussion of the equivalents of the *-ende* participles, but it may be useful to call attention to the fact that the *-ende* forms used substantively form part of a larger group of adjectives occurring in an absolute function. In this larger group there may be word-class conformity between Danish and English if the adjectives refer to a whole class of individuals. Thus *de blinde* corresponds to 'the blind' *de fattige* to 'the poor', *de stærke* to 'the strong'. In examples like 'the land of the free', 'the sleep of the just', and 'Blessed are the meek' the English adjectives are rendered by Danish adjectives. But sometimes English has available both an adjective and a noun with the same form: 'an intellectual pursuit' - 'she is an intellectual'; and where that is the case, reference to a whole class requires the use of the English noun in the plural. Thus, corresponding to *de intellektuelle* English has 'the intellectuals'. Further examples are *de indfødte*: 'the natives'; *de vilde*: 'the savages'; *de progressive*: 'the progressives'; *de sorte*: 'the Blacks'; *de liberale*: 'the Liberals' (as a party-political term); *de grønne* (the new party): 'the Greens'; *hans samtidige*: 'his contemporaries'.

2. *-isk* in Danish Adjectives of Foreign Origin and its English Equivalents

When looking for the English equivalents of Danish adjectives ending in *-isk*, like *kritisk, teoretisk, systematisk*, or *økonomisk* the translator is in most cases faced with a choice between a form ending in *-ic* or *-ical*. This choice tends to engender doubt or bewilderment, and it may therefore be useful to list the various possibilities.

2.1. In one group of English adjectives only the long form is fully current today. This is true of *chemical, critical, cynical, grammatical, hypothetical, identical, mathematical, physical, sceptical*, and *statistical*, though the corresponding short forms may occur very occasionally, especially in more or less technical use. Thus *cynic* and *sceptic*, which are predominantly nouns, may appear in adjectival function referring to these two schools of Greek philosophy.

2.2. A second group is made up of forms ending in *-ic*, for instance *Arabic, artistic, athletic, Catholic, chaotic, choleric, chronic, civic, dramatic, energetic, romantic, Semitic*, and *systematic*. It should be noted that the corresponding adverbs end in *-ally*: *artistically, romantically*, etc. Only *politic* (= 'prudent', thus semantically distinct from *political*) and *public* form adverbs by the addition of *-ly*: *politicly, publicly* (though American English also has the form *publically*).

2.3. A third group contains adjectives that alternate between *-ic* and *-ical*, the two forms being used interchangeably: *fanatic(al), pedagogic(al), strategic(al), syntactic(al)*, and *theoretic(al)*.

2.4. A fourth group consists of adjectives with two forms that differ more or less in meaning: *classic - classical, comic - comical, economic - economical, historic - historical, magic - magical, poetic - poetical*, and *stoic - stoical*.

These pairs are largely differentiated semantically through the collocations that they form part of. Thus we speak of *a classic example of megalomania*, but of *classical literature and music*; of *a comic actor* (an actor performing in comedy), but of *a comical* ('funny') *hat. Economic* pairs with the noun *economics*, so that we may refer to *our economic relations with another country*; *economical* mainly relates to *economy* in the sense of 'money-saving' - hence *an economical housekeeper. Historic means* 'important in history', so that *a historic meeting* means a meeting for which there is documentation; however, both forms are used indiscriminately in a grammatical term: *the historic(al) present*. There is less to choose between the members of the last three pairs; see for instance *A Dictionary of Modern English Usage* by H.W. Fowler, second edition revised by E. Gowers (Oxford 1965).

2.5. There is, finally, a group of terms relating to politics, ideology, etc. They are nouns like *anarchist, capitalist, communist, imperialist, nationalist, nihilist, opportunist, royalist, socialist, terrorist,* and *zionist,* which are also used as classifying adjectives. Besides, there exist longer forms in *-ic: anarchistic, socialistic,* etc., of which it may be said that they are descriptive adjectives that occur less frequently than the shorter forms. The two sets thus convey slightly different shades of meaning: *a socialist country* places that country in a certain category, while *a socialistic country* suggests the characteristics of such a country. Classifying adjectives are non-gradable, i.e. they cannot be modified by adverbs, while descriptive adjectives are gradable, so that it makes sense to refer to *the less socialistic countries.* For this group, then, a choice has to be made between forms ending in *-ist* and *-istic.* Note that *revisionist* only occurs in the short form.

In one case there is a choice between *-ian* and *-ist*: *Marxian -Marxist*; these two adjectives appear to be used indiscriminately. Corresponding to *dystopia, subtopia,* and *utopia* only one adjectival form is available: *dystopian, subtopian,* and *utopian.*

3. Danish Compound Nouns and their English Equivalents

The Danish type of nominal compound that will be taken as our point of departure here consists of noun + noun and may be exemplified by words like *kammermusik, nervesammenbrud, tommelfingerregel,* and *pigeskole.* In most cases the English equivalents of such words consist of two (or sometimes more) elements forming various patterns, though this is not invariably the case. For instance the Danish compound *turistfører* corresponds to English 'guide', *blodåre* to 'vein'. Inversely, some English compounds can be translated by a Danish simplex; this applies for instance to 'framework' (*ramme*) and 'wallpaper' (*tapet*). But there are plenty of examples illustrating the normal translation equivalence: Danish compounds having English equivalents that consist of two (or more) words, and these will be our concern in what follows. They may be divided into different types.

Type 1a. In a number of cases Danish and English have exactly the same type of compound, namely singular noun + singular noun written solid. This is true of examples like *hjemland*: 'homeland'; *spiseske*: 'tablespoon'; and *tandbørste*: 'toothbrush'. It should be noted, however, that while Danish obeys the fairly rigid convention of writing compounds in one word, there is much vacillation in English; here we shall follow the orthography found in *Everyman's English Pronouncing Dictionary* (fourteenth edition, London 1977), and we shall include under Type 1a examples of the two other English spellings: *bordkniv*: 'table-knife'; *gæstehåndklæde*: 'guest-towel'; *magtelite*: 'power élite'; *rentesats*: 'interest rate'; *terrorbalance*: 'terror balance' (note that the last two English examples alternate with Type 3); *sympatistrejke*: 'sympathy strike' (here there is alternation with Type 2).

Type 1b. Here the first element of the English compound is in the plural: *indkomstpolitik*: 'incomes policy'; *ankeprotokol*: 'complaints book'.

Type 2. Danish noun + noun, corresponding to English adjective + noun. This is a type with numerous members, e.g. *arvesynden*: 'original sin'; *et nervesammenbrud*: 'a nervous breakdown'; *en stammekrig*: 'a tribal war'; *ønsketænkning*: 'wishful thinking'. It may be noted that the adjectival element may be either a participle, as in 'a neighbouring country' and 'planned economy', or an adjective that is often of Greek or Latin origin: 'a gastric ulcer', 'solar energy'.

There is occasional vacillation between Types 1a and 2: the 'sympathy strike' listed above alternates with 'a sympathetic strike', and one finds both 'a pot plant' and 'a potted plant', 'a sex role' and 'a sexual role'.

Type 3. Danish noun + noun, corresponding to English noun + *of* + noun: (*en kolos på*) *lerfødder*: '('an image with) feet of clay'; *svedperler*: 'beads of perspiration'; *en tommelfingerregel*: 'a rule of thumb'; *bevisbyrden*: 'the burden of proof'; *en hensigtserklæring*: 'a declaration of intent'. English examples like these are exclusively postmodified, but in some cases there is alternation between Types 1a and 3: 'an interest rate' and 'the terror balance' alternate with 'a rate of interest' and 'the balance of terror', and similarly we find either 'a battle order' or ' an order of battle', 'a growth rate' or 'a rate of growth'. Stylistically there is a tendency for a Type 3 form to occur at first mention in a given context, followed by a Type 1 form at second mention, as illustrated in this example:

After hearing the circumstances which would for the basis of the case for *a declaration of nullity*, everyone consulted agreed that this case was simple and that *a nullity declaration* would be given... (Christopher Sykes, *Evelyn Waugh. A Bibliography*, Penguin 1977, p.188)

It may be added that Type 1 is clearly on the increase. Instead of normal forms like 'birds of prey', 'fear of death', and 'feelings of guilt', one may sometimes come across 'prey birds', 'death fear', and 'guilt feelings'. It is all the more striking that Amnesty International should have introduced the expression 'a prisoner of conscience' (*en samvittighedsfange*) as recently as in 1961; the model must have been one of the firmly entrenched Type 3 members, namely 'a prisoner of war'.

Occasionally there is competition between Types 2 and 3: we may refer to 'an analytic method' or to 'a method of analysis'.

In at least one case British and American English differ: British English only uses Type 3 in 'a house of cards', while according to Webster (1961) American English besides this makes use of the Type 1 form 'a cardhouse'.

Type 4. Danish noun + noun, corresponding to English noun in the genitive + noun. This is a type with comparatively few members, among them *et dukkehus*: 'a doll's house'; *en hvepserede*: 'a hornet's nest'; *en pigeskole*: 'a girl's school'; *modermælk*: 'mother's milk'; *et dødningehoved*: 'a death's head'; *Djævleøen*: '(the) Devil's Island'; *en trykfejl*: 'a printer's error'. Occasionally one may find representatives of Types 4 and 1 combined, as in 'pheasant's and ostrich feathers'. In 'landsman': *landkrabbe* the first component is an old genitive that is not indicated as such by the use of the apostrophe.

It appears from these comparisons that there is a greater degree of choice in English than in Danish: *-ende* corresponds to *-ing, -y, -ent, -er,* or *-ive; -isk* to *-ic, -ical, -ist,* or *-ian*; and Danish noun + noun compounds have four English equivalents. What this article has tried to do is to call attention to the existence of these choices, while it is of course impossible to provide exhaustive lists of the members of the different groups and types.

If there is greater diversity in English than in Danish, it is due both to its extensive use of affixes and to its large-scale adoption of loanwords. What this implies from the translator's point of view is that when he moves from Danish to English he is confronted with greater problems of selection in these areas than when he moves in the opposite direction.

The Sad Story about the Children who were Left by their Grandparents

Flemming Olsen

1. Introduction

An Englishman seeing that headline will believe that he is going to read a fairy tale of the more sinister sort. However, if the sentence is the outcome of a Danish Grammar School[1] pupil's translation efforts, the odds are that the reference is to a quite harmless babysitter situation: under the influence of Danish (and perhaps German), the translator has used a wrong preposition, viz. 'by' for 'with'.

So an Englishman would not understand the sentence as the sender intended it to be understood. One of the cruxes of foreign language teaching is how to prevent pupils from committing that kind of 'wrong parallel' error in their use of the target language.

It is immediately obvious that the usual panacea of English language teaching, viz. steeping the learner in as much idiomatic English as possible in order to make him pick up things 'instinctively', is insufficient in this case: the sentence is correct and comprehensible English, and many a Danish speaker would probably not be aware of the misunderstanding unless he had it pointed out to him.

However, any Danish teacher of English who is worth his salt will know that the translation of the Danish preposition *hos* poses considerable problems for Grammar School pupils. The reason is not only that there is more than one English equivalent, but also that the prepositions that are used, viz. 'at', 'with', 'of', 'in', mean other things as well in Danish. The pupils are obviously confused by the fact that there is not one English word for the Danish *hos*.

How can the teacher make his pupils steer clear of the trap? The first thing is to make them aware of the problem, and one way of doing that is by practising, or making his pupils practise, frequent juxtaposition of the two languages or systematic translation, hoping to open their eyes to the danger.

Are the teacher's hopes fulfilled? Do the results justify the efforts? These are two central questions that will be debated, together with some others, in the rest of this article.

2. The Classroom

The classroom is in many respects comparable to a pedagogic laboratory: observations are made and hypotheses tested by the teacher, who will take cognizance of events and developments and make current revisions of his teaching practice. This latter point makes it plausible that the different fields of teaching, including translation, should be subjected to continuous critical analysis.

On the other hand, the pupils are more than mere guinea pigs, and the results of the analyses cannot pretend to have the exactitude of scientific data. That is why the conclusions are necessarily far more tentative and subjective than those reached by science.

What matters is classroom expediency rather than the confirmation of pre-conceived theories. So 'workshop' is probably a more appropriate word than 'laboratory' to characterize the interaction between teachers and pupils in the classroom. Several factors contribute to keeping the teaching going, e.g. examination requirements, the pupils' varying degrees of intelligence and motivation, and the teacher's professional and pedagogic competence and experience.

Both the written and the oral *studentereksamen* in English include translation as part of the assignment. The argument usually given for the combination of 'free production' and translation at the written exam is that whereas the former encourages independent writing on the pupil's part, the translation serves as a useful corrective because it makes stricter demands on precision than does 'free production'.

It is true that the Grammar School Reform that came into force in August 1988 reduces the translation part of the assignment rather more than the 'free production' part. On the other hand, translation from English into Danish has been preserved virtually unchanged as part of the oral examination.

One fundamental question is: do we 'do' translation in our everyday classroom work for the simple reason that translation is a discipline that is tested in the examination room? That is hard to believe: since examination requirements were obviously not instituted by God, it seems reasonable to assume that translation, from English as well as into English, is believed to be inherently valuable.

The pupils referred to in this article are a mixed bag, covering Grammar School beginners of approximately 16 as well as Sixth Formers in their last term, i.e. young people aged about 19. But the category also ranges from the rather mediocre to the truly brilliant ones. Accordingly, generalizations will have to be made, and it goes without saying that the generalizations will have to be taken with a grain of salt.

It would seem to be a reasonable assumption that a person's ability to translate is a function of his linguistic competence, i.e. his mastery of his mother tongue combined with a sensitivity to what happens when words are connected into sentences, or when one word in a context is replaced by another. That kind of competence is surely not unconnected with the person's ability to collect and marshall facts. Not only is that talent differently developed in different individuals, but in this particular case matters are further complicated by the fact that some teenagers have not fully developed that ability until they have reached the age when they are on the point of leaving Grammar School.

Those whom we conventionally call intelligent are able to cope with virtually any problem, thanks to the way in which they tackle things. The question is whether translation is of some help to those who do not shine at foreign language acquisition.

In some respects, it does seem to be useful. Let's take the teaching of grammar as an illustration: most teachers find it rewarding, when dealing with grammar on more than the most superficial level, to make current references to, and comparisons with, the pupils' native language. Some teachers even 'do' all grammatical topics in Danish. The reason is twofold. First, it saves time. That argument can be used to justify translation at all levels and within all the fields of the teaching. The point here is not so much whether it would be feasible to do the grammar teaching in English, for of course it would. Only, the teacher would be required to take great care in preparing the problems to be treated and in ensuring that there was the necessary progression. No, it is rather that since we do not have unlimited time at our disposal - after all, none of us live to be 200 - squinting grammar is a practical time-saver.

The second reason for making occasional references to the pupils' mother tongue is that teenagers tend to find points of grammar fairly theoretical. Experience shows that juxtaposition with analogous cases in Danish provides the problems with flesh and blood. To some pupils, then, translation is a shortcut to understanding.

The overall aim is to teach the pupils a reasonable competence in English, a competence including a judicious mixture of correctness and fluency. It is probably true to say that there is a need these days for a better balance between the two: over the last decades, fluency has been in danger of degenerating, teachers clapping their hands enthusiastically if only pupils deigned to open their mouths. Can translation be useful in redressing the balance between correctness and fluency?

One of the purposes of translation is to call the pupils' attention to some of the more common, and potentially dangerous, pitfalls seen from a Danish point of view. Or, to put it differently, the object is to reduce, and to go some way towards eliminating, the interference from Danish. It may seem paradoxical, but my experience shows that translation does reduce some of the interference.

Ideally, the teaching should also make the pupils good language learners. Among the qualities that go to make up such a learner, two are of particular relevance here, viz. a readiness to let one's hair down and commit oneself, and a considerable amount of what may be called 'ego permeability', which implies a realization that one's own linguistic system is not the only valid or imaginable one, and a concomitant willingness to be influenced by the patterns of the target language.

Is translation helpful when it comes to meeting either, or perhaps both, of those requirements?

3. Translation

The word translation has been used rather loosely several times in this article. It is appropriate to specify the senses of the word that are relevant in a classroom situation. First, it may refer to a rendering, in either of the languages, of a fairly long passage originally verbalized in the other (e.g. a Danish translation text, or a Shakespeare monologue). Secondly, it may denote the fact that the teacher quickly supplies the Danish (or English) equivalent for an English (or Danish) word or idiom in order for the teaching to keep its pace.

It seems to be a natural thing for any learner of a foreign language to draw parallels between his mother tongue and the target language. But of course the question is whether the medium of that juxtaposition needs to be translation.

Boys and girls in their late teens are in a state of budding awareness of their own language and of the use that can be made of it. Their relation to the concept of language makes it a profitable pursuit for them to familiarize themselves with other languages than their mother tongue. And they are still so linguistically inexperienced that they will sometimes be surprised to see that all languages do not structure the world in the same way. But, for Danes, the basis of comparison is of course, inevitably, Danish. Part of the fun of learning e.g. English consists in discovering that there is no one-to-one correspondence between the vocabularies of Danish and English: it is as difficult to find a Danish equivalent for 'sanity' as to find an English one for *hyggelig*.

3.1. Contrastive Analysis

Contrastive analysis is an extremely fruitful method where language learning and teaching is concerned. On a larger scale, it enables learners to see that two languages are the expressions of two different cultures: the Danes use the equivalent of 'thank you' in various collocations far more frequently than do the English. On the other hand, no Dane understands the associations surrounding the English word 'precedent' unless they are explained to him.

The new Grammar School *bekendtgørelse* for English stipulates that pupils 'should be enabled to understand similarities and dissimilarities between the world of their own experience and the world they meet in English-speaking cultures'. Familiarization with a foreign language teaches the pupils that the Danish world picture is not necessarily of universal validity: it is something of an eye-opener for pupils to be told that, in English, red and pink are two different colours, whereas the Danish counterparts are two nuances of the same colour. Equally interesting are the cases where words are formally almost identical, but semantically different: the Danish 'eventuelt' means 'possibly', which the English 'eventually' does not. And the modal verbs of the two languages show a great degree of formal coalescence: *kan - kunne*, 'can - could'; *skal - skulle*, 'shall - should'; *vil - ville*, 'will - would'. However, semantically, the modal verbs are widely different in the two languages.

The really stimulating cases are the 'untranslatable' words, which means words for which no (single) corresponding word exists in the other language so that periphrasis or explanation is necessary: such words force the learner to modify or widen his world view. Thus, there is no single Danish equivalent for the mixture of firm promise and responsibility implied in the English 'commitment'; the word *pligt* is sometimes used, but that word is also used to render the meaning of the English 'duty', which is, of course, totally different from 'commitment'.

A contrastive approach may - more or less gently, it is true - induce pupils to devote particular energy to phenomena that can be said to be objectively difficult, for example in cases where a language seems to go its own way. A case in point is the use of the simple and progressive tenses of the verbs in English, which is extremely complicated for a Dane (and probably for any non-native speaker) to learn.

3.2. The Nature Method

The discussion about whether or not to juxtapose the mother tongue and the target language inevitably brings up several of the points that, some decades ago, characterized the debate about learning a language by the so-called 'nature method'. The doctrine of that method had the force of a revelation because it was disarmingly simple: the same procedure was to be used when learning a second language as a child uses when picking up his mother tongue.

The assumption was that if learners were steeped in a considerable amount of, for instance, idiomatic English, a kind of osmosis would take place in their minds so that they would instinctively appropriate the patterns, which would spring forth spontaneously when needed. The use of the mother tongue was banned as being heretical and 'against nature'.

However, it should not be forgotten that, for all its claim to be ideologically untainted, the 'nature method' practised implicit juxtaposition, or even translation, wholeheartedly: a Danish teacher employing the 'nature method' would always dwell with particular care on the cases where Danish learners were liable to put their foot in it unless forewarned because they would spontaneously transfer Danish patterns to English. The teacher, giving his pupils a significant look, would raise his voice and repeat, 'Where is the money? It is on the table'. The point is that the Danish equivalent for 'money', viz. *penge* is the plural, hence the teacher's histrionic efforts.

However, a sentence of the type, 'I want to buy a new house' would pass virtually unnoticed because, in that case, the constructions of the two languages are identical; indeed a word-by-word translation from Danish would produce the correct English counterpart.

The two sentences just quoted are equally interesting or uninteresting for a native English speaker. But the point is that, by using procedures like the one outlined above, teaching by the 'nature method' tended to become implicitly contrastive, which, however, its practitioners would indignantly deny.

More generally, it would seem that the belief in the existence of a sort of latent foreign language competence that could be activated by being stimulated in the foreign language was somewhat exaggerated. Thus it is characteristic that the results of the 'nature method' were markedly better for Danish learners of English than of, for example, French, not to say Russian, because Danish and English have a large number of words and structures in common. It was the fortuitous similarity between two languages rather than a native human talent that yielded the astonishing results.

The question that poses itself acutely is the following one: if the 'nature method', which claimed to be *the* way of learning a language, including the mother tongue, could not leave juxtaposition and implicit translation entirely out of account, would it not be an equally 'natural' thing - and more straight-forward pedagogy - to let the teaching become explicitly contrastive?

3.3. The Usefulness of Translation

The teacher who takes it for granted that his pupils will spontaneously 'internalize' the correct solutions will, in the great majority of cases, face some disappointments. My experience has taught me that explicit juxtaposition of the two languages is a necessity. Translation is not a cure-all in foreign language teaching, but it is one means of making similarities and dissimilarities stand out in clear relief. And, more than that, it is arguable that the most intimate knowledge of, and familiarity with, a foreign language and its underlying culture arise as a consequence of occasional translation of different types of texts using that language as their medium. So the inclusion of translation in the examination requirements for English at Grammar School level is, in my opinion, both a natural and a sensible thing.

In what way, or ways, is translation helpful? To what extent is the improvement in the pupils' achievements as they proceed in Grammar School due to the fact that translation is a regular ingredient of the teaching?

A definite answer cannot be given for the very good reason that teachers have to obey the laws of the country. Accordingly, no control groups who are exempted from translation can ever be set up, which means that really reliable comparisons can never be established. So it remains uncertain whether the reduction of errors reflected in the pupils' oral and written performances is caused by the simple fact that they read more and more English. And who knows if the same improvement might not be achieved by a more intensive teaching of English *in English* only? Only, everything goes to show that such teaching would consume an enormous amount of time if the teacher were to ensure and check that all the pupils fully understood every aspect.

3.4. Transference from Danish

How much damage is likely to be done if we chose, on principle, to avoid all kinds of translation or juxtaposition between the two languages? If nothing but English were used in the classroom, would a Danish Grammar School pupil plunge into a North Sea variant of language, a hybrid of English on a recognizable Danish substratum?

Needless to say, it would be most unfortunate if the native English listener's attention were diverted from the message because he had to focus unduly on the form. Of course, the threshold of acceptance varies from one listener to another, but, in a very general way, it can be said that the English tend to be fairly tolerant in such matters. Much depends on the kind of mistake that is committed: surveys have shown that the rate of misunderstanding where vocabulary is concerned is six to eight times higher than in the case of incorrect grammar. But then again, repeated errors of grammar may make the conversation break down for other reasons, e.g. bewilderment or irritation on the part of the native listener, for all his nation's proverbial tolerance.

A Dane who has not been repeatedly warned will spontaneously say 'When I was on the hospital...', and no Englishman will seriously believe that the speaker had unaccountably been placed on the roof. By the same token, all English listeners are likely to swallow the grammatical blunder in 'all my books were disappeared' without batting an eyelid. The meaning, of course, is crystal clear, and English speakers will boggle at the type of mistake mentioned in this paragraph only if prodded.

Typical Danicisms like 'the man there is rich', using 'there' as a relative pronoun on the analogy of Danish usage, and 'when they came out of the church their car was stolen' (instead of 'had been stolen') will be immediately understood by the addressee: the point about the man is his money, and the relevant fact about the car is that it was gone, not the time when it disappeared. That means that the part of the message containing the 'heavy' information value does come across.

More tricky cases are the following ones because they are instances of correct English, which means that a native speaker will not suspect that something is wrong but will take the sentences to be intended to mean what they mean to him. 'Two years later, Emily suddenly became a younger sister': Danes have great difficulty in sorting out the correct uses of 'get' and 'become'. 'No more, thank you, I had a better dinner yesterday, you see': comparative forms of adjectives are used in Danish also to indicate a fairly high degree. So what the speaker means is that he has no appetite since he was treated to a grand dinner the previous day; not, as the English listener would take it, that yesterday's dinner was actually preferable to the one he is being given now.

A Dane might very well say 'I decided to take over and find the pop group that had recorded the music', transferring the Danish 'tage' in the sense of 'go', 'travel' directly to English. The Dane, then, intended to make a journey, e.g. abroad, to try to discover the identity of the group. An Englishman would of course believe that the speaker intended to take charge of a project.

Examples might be multiplied, but a sufficient number has been given to show that word-by-word translations from Danish into English can be arranged on a scale of ascending trickiness: at one end we find fairly innocent ones like 'I wonder how many people there will answer his letters'. At the other extreme, we find misleading, potentially disastrous, ones like 'She goes home', meaning 'She's a housewife' (i.e. does not work outside the home).

Of course the conversation situation will soon eliminate most of the minor misunderstandings. But the point is that the really unfortunate ones may create an embarrassing 'understanding gap' between the two speakers. And the situation becomes far more problematic if the two participants are not face to face but communicate on the phone or in writing.

There is probably little disagreement that such mistakes have to be pointed out to most pupils if they are to avoid them. Only a small minority have the capacity of assimilating such points spontaneously from what they read or hear. Any experienced teacher will of course know where the genuine pitfalls are, and he will warn his pupils accordingly. There are several ways of teaching pupils to avoid catastrophes, e.g. repetition, explanation in English, and translation. It is my impression that translation not infrequently makes assurance double sure.

3.5. Translation and Understanding

Does an average Danish Grammar School pupil understand an English text better if he or she is made to translate it into Danish? Everything hinges on the meaning attributed to the word 'understand'. It must be remembered that, in the classroom, the pupil must show his understanding in behavioural terms, e.g. by his ability to demonstrate, identify, choose, and combine. If 'understanding' means nothing more than what can be demonstrated by a reasonably plausible summary, surely it would be patently absurd to switch to Danish. But 'understanding' a fairly transparent short story, not to say a poem, may be, indeed most often is, something more complicated than what can be tested in a mere summary: it may be a question of accounting for the interaction of plot and character, or for the specific mood evoked by a particular metaphor. In such cases, having recourse to the mother tongue in the form of translation, and occasionally also discussion, is a practical, sometimes necessary, procedure because often the pupils will not possess a sufficient variety of English idioms to be able to pinpoint their reactions and attitudes.

Admittedly, translation *per se* is often not enough to show the teacher whether especially the weak pupil has understood a passage properly. Frequently additional comments or explanations are needed, but it is obvious that such a pupil would be even worse off without a translation to begin with.

Of course a further danger, of which any teacher should be acutely aware, is that, by furnishing the word, the teacher may also force an attitude on the pupils. Is a pupil's hesitation due to the fact that he has not got the English word, or is he simply unable to get to grips with the text? Can't he see that the text is ironic, or is he just unaware of the correct form of the English adjective? Here again, occasional shuttlings between the two languages may be beneficial, the pupils' range of words being naturally greater in their native language than in a foreign one.

Finally, occasional or regular translation may strengthen the better pupil's sense of style, both in English and in Danish. Even if a pupil is told that 'solace' is a fairly formal word, he may still be left more or less in the dark. If the Danish stylistic equivalent, *husvalelse*, is provided, he may suddenly get a clearer idea of the associations surrounding the English word. The same thing may happen in the case of stylistic designations like 'learned', 'obsolete', 'colloquial', etc.

3.6. Translation and the Pupils' Mother Tongue

It is sometimes argued that translation into Danish tests the pupils' command of Danish just as much as their grasp of the English text. But, surely, that argument works both ways: translation into English will test the pupils' understanding of the Danish text plus their command of English idiom, and who can possibly mind that?

There is an added advantage that should not be overlooked, viz. that translation of English texts may contribute to increasing and refining the pupils' Danish vocabulary. The implications are worthy of consideration: all experience goes to show that the person who masters 5,000 words fares better in the world than one who masters only 500.

Indirectly, then, translation may counteract many pupils' conviction that Danish is a language containing far fewer words than English, and it may reinforce their sense of what it means to be Danish. Also, it is my impression that, to many pupils, the word is an eye-opener to the thing or the concept. So the more words they are in possession of, the better they will be qualified to pick the locks of the world.

No doubt translation exercises and regular comparisons between the two languages establish some inhibitions in the pupils. The purpose is, of course, to prevent pupils falling into traps presented by words that are seemingly identical in the two languages. To take one example, much time will be devoted to determining the exact shades of meaning of the English word 'should' compared to those of its Danish counterpart *skulle*.

The question is to what extent the many warnings will clip the wings of those who are bold and willing to commit themselves. At first sight, the danger seems a very real one: many intelligent pupils are also perfectionists, and it would certainly be deplorable if the teaching inhibited them to such an extent that they would never venture off the beaten track. The weak pupils need support: rules are helpful, and so are translations and juxtapositions. The dedicated teacher feels it incumbent on him to devote much energy to helping them. The attitude is justified by the experiential fact that the brighter ones can manage without being spoonfed all the time. They seem to know instinctively which of the teacher's warnings are relevant for their purposes, and they sort them out accordingly. Occasional squinting translation does not seem to deter competent pupils from sticking out their necks.

3.7. Free Production

But, it may be asked, are the idioms, etc. that he is taught in translation in any way useful for the pupil when he is on his own? Does he produce better English spontaneously because he has 'done' some translation? The question can be put differently: to what extent and how do translation exercises influence the pupils' 'free production'?

There is little doubt that the thing called 'free production' needs further analysis. Many teachers consider it an ideal because it is held to be more independent, hence more mature and valuable, than, for example, translation. But how many Danes will actually need a real competence in 'free production' in English - unless, of course, they are going to be students of English? It is true that they may have to write a letter now and then, or to carry on a conversation about other subjects than the weather or the make of their car. Some of them may have to write articles or give lectures in English in a professional capacity, but in such circumstances the technical terminology, with which they will be entirely familiar, is sure to form the backbone of their contributions.

The purpose of the preceding lines was not to disparage the thing called 'free production'. But, first, there is a very great probability that the number of pupils who will be engaged in some kind of translation in their later careers far exceeds the number of those who will be required to 'do' 'free production' above a fairly humdrum level.

Secondly, and no less importantly, the term 'free production' is something of a misnomer: hardly any Danish Grammar School pupil is able to conjure up spontaneously a string of words and sentences in beautiful and impeccable English. Since divine intervention is out of the question, 'free production' comes to be synonymous with more or less *conditioned* production: the pupil does not have at his command a spectrum of English idioms enabling him to hold forth on a variety of subjects. The thoughts that he may have on a given subject will, in the great majority of cases, be verbalized in Danish: only very rarely does a pupil spontaneously 'think' in English or hit on an English turn of phrase as the first and natural thing.

What this means is that, in Grammar School terms, 'free production' is not synonymous with uninhibited roving around the fields of the foreign language. There are, inevitably, lacunae in the pupils' vocabulary, and frequently they may have to consult a dictionary. It is a truism to state that in not a few cases the dictionary will be a Danish-English one. An English-English dictionary may admittedly be helpful as far as collocations and syntactical constructions are concerned. But if a pupil is stuck for one or more words he will usually quite instinctively go back to Danish: he does not possess a store of English idioms that he can draw on at his discretion.

As I see it, 'free production' is not the opposite of, or a more sophisticated variant of, translation. Rather, the two should be awarded parity of esteem for they are two equally respectable aspects of a pupil's acquisition and treatment of a foreign language. It is wide of the mark to pretend that Danish Grammar School pupils' 'free production' in a language that is not their mother tongue is synonymous with healthy creativity, indeed an almost artistic display, whereas translation fetters the boldness of their flights with the trammels of pedantry and cripples the God-inspired sublimity of their linguistic genius.

A weak pupil's 'free production' will often be a pathetic performance for the very reason that his Danish resources are so depressingly scarce. And the productions of the more diffuse kind of pupil will often be a very peculiar experience indeed for the teacher. It is a well-known fact, which is certainly not unrelated to what has just been said, that the great majority of pupils prefer to be given a limited and reasonably well-defined assignment: their pet aversion is an invitation to 'write on any topic you like'.

The 'free productions' of some pupils give the teacher repeated thrills of pleasure. Those of other pupils are cascades of nonsense couched in a parody of any linguistic structure.

Of course 'free production' does not imply total freedom for the pupils in the sense that they suddenly rise above the rules of grammar and are allowed to suspend traditional syntactical structures, etc. 'Free production' is, one could say, an English causerie on a given topic, which involves advantages and disadvantages. Among the latter may be mentioned the following problem: in a Danish translation piece, phenomena like coordination and subordination, cohesion and coherence, etc. are given in the text. However, in cases where the pupil is to write independently, he will have to supply his own suggestions for such features. A person's 'free production' in English is largely determined by his command of Danish - or perhaps it is more correct to say his command of language. It seems that a person is possessed of a talent for language rather than for *a* language: those who are admirably competent in their mother tongue freely transfer their talent to another language. And those who are really poor at Danish are able to make only mechanical and uninspired English 'free' performances, unless they are helped a bit on the way, that is.

It is my experience that some translation practice will enable some of the not strikingly bright pupils to acquire a sense of how a sentence can be structured, how transitions can be made, and where full stops are appropriate, etc. Thus translation exercises may help them avoid more than 'mere' blunders of grammar. Thanks to the teacher's indefatigable comparisons, juxtapositions, and repetitions, some pupils are actually enabled to pick up some odd bits of relevant material. As a matter of fact, far from being a restrictive element, translation will not infrequently turn out to be a safety net under the lesser lights of the classroom.

So translation is not a closed circuit: the teaching of it does have some repercussions in, and consequences for, the pupils' mastery of the target language, which becomes discernible when they are invited to test the scope of their command of it.

The postulate put forward in the previous paragraph can be supported by evidence from my own experience: if I ask Grammar School beginners (i.e. pupils who have been taught English for five or six years) to indulge in 'free composition', Danish interference will be considerably more pervasive, also with the brighter category of pupils, than if I start with some contrastive exercises, e.g. in the form of elementary translation, and afterwards proceed to assign some 'free production' papers to them.

4. The Pupils

It is of course a Utopian wish to be able to engage and motivate all pupils in all classes in all aspects of the teaching, but the teacher should explore every avenue to include as many pupils as possible in the teaching process.

In my experience, regular translation practice is useful also as a pedagogic device: as was pointed out earlier in this article, the weak pupils look upon translation, be it into English or Danish, as a reassuring factor. They have a feeling that once a text has been translated some problems have been properly pigeon-holed, if not solved. To the unimaginative ones, translation is a *pièce de résistance* of their learning process, and their achievements are usually perceptibly better in translation than when they are left to their own devices. Even those who are above average will be kindly disposed towards translation, not only because the texts are often inherently valuable and not mechanical drills, but also because they seem to enjoy shuttling between two languages.

If no translation or comparison were ever used, there is a very great likelihood that the pupils would, intuitively, draw parallels with Danish. An analogous case is grammar, where it is a fact that pupils tend to make rules or generalizations whether the teacher encourages rule-making or not. In my experience, juxtaposition with their mother tongue is some pupils' way of making their language learning less chaotic and more systematic - one might be tempted to call it a kind of self-defence.

Some pupils develop considerable skills of juxtaposition. The trouble is, however, that if such parallels remain hidden they are uncontrollable, and they may not be such as the teacher would have recommended. The pupils will show the rightness or wrongness of their inferences when they speak or write, which means that correction will follow their performances. Even if such correction does not have to be pedantic knuckle-rapping, a good many pupils may find that they would have been able to avoid at least some of the pitfalls if they had been duly forewarned.

Besides, there is little doubt that a considerable number of pupils would feel let down or lost if the teacher consistently refused to use translation. They would mainly be the pupils who long for the safety of system and clarity and who think that those two aspects are provided by translation. Admittedly, a teacher may find it useful sometimes to undeceive such pupils by demonstrating that in quite a few cases the clarity provided by translation, alone and unassisted by explanation, may be of a fairly dubious character. But then again, causing the underpinnings of the pupils' confidence to collapse is not a virtue in itself.

Some pupils (and perhaps teachers) look upon translation as a learning process whereas others - teachers as well as pupils - regard it as a test of their understanding. Many of them will have a clear perception of the training aspect because they know that in their later careers they will have to practise some kind of translation. Specific terms and turns of phrase will come quite naturally when they start working in banks, shipping offices or industrial enterprises. So what they endeavour to pick up in Grammar School is some basic competence within the areas of grammar, syntax and idiom.

To the majority of adult Danes, English is a second language which they use not only when travelling abroad but frequently also in their jobs. To such people, there is no unbridgeable gulf between English and Danish, and they find it natural, even necessary, to switch from one of the languages to the other.

Surely, it would be absurd if the education system did not prepare the pupils for their later experiences (and needs), not in the sense of teaching them translation theory but by giving them some practical instances of how the two languages behave.

Besides, it should be emphasized that only a small percentage of the pupils actually dislike the element of testing that is discreetly employed not only in translation, but in all the daily give-and-take of the classroom. In fact, many pupils use translation exercises as a more or less explicit means of self-testing, noticing with no little satisfaction their progress in the mastery of the foreign language. Translation stimulates them to make fertile inductive generalizations, for example as regards the distribution of the indefinite pronouns 'some' and 'any' and their derived forms: the distinction between the conceptual content of the two words does exist in Danish, only it tends to be blurred.

5. The Material

The texts that are used as translation material from Danish into English are cautiously adapted specimens of Danish standard prose. Obviously not any type of text will do: literary passages are too difficult, and dialect or substandard texts, or texts with an exclusively technical bias, are irrelevant because the aim in Grammar School is not to cultivate narrow specialization.

There are further limitations: long passages of Danish prose that show little or no deviation from English as regards syntax, idiom, etc. are less interesting because they are virtually devoid of any element of testing. And finally, the target language, in this case English, is taken into consideration in the sense that the Danish text should be translatable into English: Grammar School pupils should be able to make idiomatic English out of their translation without unreasonable demands being made on their linguistic competence.

The latter point is not without importance, and it is amply illustrated by the difficulty bordering on impossibility of giving an idiomatic English version of a Danish text which is meant to be translated into, for example, German.

What this means is that the Danish text will be tailored to its purpose, viz. testing the pupils' competence in specimens of not unduly specialized English standard language.

Inevitably, then, the translation pieces will contain tests - of grammar, idiom, vocabulary, and syntax. The emphasis will naturally be on the points where automatic transference from Danish is liable to produce unfortunate results, e.g. the position of adverbs, or the distribution of countable and uncountable nouns (the system is known in Danish, but the affiliation of nouns to the two groups is different).

But the tests will also include problems that are more specifically English, such as the correct use of adjectives and adverbs, which seems to be a kind of social marker for a native English speaker. Or instances of simple and progressive tense forms of the verbs, which is something utterly unknown in Danish, for which reason a Danish speaker will have to resort to various kinds of paraphrase to clarify the distinction.

So the texts contain pitfalls for the pupils - pitfalls which, if not avoided, will lead to misunderstanding on the part of the recipient: not only minor and negligible flaws like 'on beforehand' or 'for three days ago' (both of them true reflections of Danish usage), but also more serious sources of communication gaps like wrong uses of 'should'.

Such 'traps' do not, of course, make up a finite number, but many of them are sure winners in Danish pupils' handling of English. A possible rule-of-thumb hierarchy might be, beginning with the most serious type of mistake: 1) vocabulary, 2) grammar (including spelling and syntax), and 3) idiom, in which latter field it is virtually impossible to establish rules, or to generalize. The position of the items on the list is determined by the degree of confusion that mistakes are likely to cause among native speakers.

An experienced teacher will know where the danger spots are, and he will know what can reasonably be expected and demanded of his pupils at different levels. He will select or arrange his materials accordingly. What we mean when we talk of a person's competence as a teacher of English is not least the extent to which he has familiarized himself with such minefields, and the talent, elegance, and efficiency with which he teaches and encourages his pupils to move in those areas, nothing daunted and reasonably unscathed.

The Danish translation text will often be a short anecdote, or extracts from a longer account, studded with warning signals that are immediately perceptible to the initiated and with which the pupils are supposed to become increasingly familiar as they progress in Grammar School. There is a good deal of stimulus and response in the discipline called 'translation' at Grammar School level. Sometimes it comes very close to being error anticipation.

It is only fair to add, though, that some pupils cannot see a trap without being seized with an irresistible desire to plunge into it, and experience shows that there are three ways of improving the standard of the really weak pupils. They are repetition, repetition, and repetition.

Of course it is easy to point the finger of scorn at such exercises and refer to the notorious fact that a native reader's conception of a Danish pupil's translation performance will frequently differ considerably from that of a Danish teacher of English. However, neither the work nor the result are as farcical as might appear at first sight.

Some decades ago, a Danish translation piece would be little more than a string of sentences illustrating so many paragraphs in the grammar books. The translation was a test of the pupil's familiarity with the grammar book rather than of his command of idiomatic English, and the resulting English version would sometimes be a most peculiar product.

However, there has been a perceptible change. Today, the Danish originals are 'purer' in the sense that they have been less tampered with. The result is that the translation pieces will also give examples of Danish idioms for which no one-to-one English correspondence exists. Accordingly, the pupils will have to draw on such resources as the teaching will have given them (including the use of dictionaries) in order to paraphrase some of the expressions so as to produce acceptable English.

Unlike the Danish translation texts, the English material normally consists of unabridged and unadapted texts, e.g. literary passages or newspaper articles. Technical or highly specialized articles are avoided, but, generally speaking, the spectrum of English translation material is wider than is the case when a Danish text is the starting-point.

The reason is not far to seek: the English curriculum includes works that were by no means intended for a Danish pupil's convenience. That is why explanation will often have to accompany translation.

The difficulty of the English texts is of course accommodated to the intellectual level of the pupils, which is another way of saying that the texts used during their three years of Grammar School will show an increasing degree of complication.

Translation theory is taught only to a very limited extent, if at all. What the pupils need is some tips that will stand them in good stead when they are faced with a text to be translated. The major point here of course is for the pupils to learn when and how to make profitable use of a dictionary, so that, for example, they do not, robot-like, invariably choose the first suggestion offered by the dictionary, irrespective of the context of 'their' word. There are other kinds of useful advice that they can benefit from, too. They should know that it is important to look at the whole passage before beginning to translate so as to get the gist of the text: help from the context is always useful, frequently invaluable. They should learn to pay attention to the sentence coordinators: 'but' introduces a contrast, 'or' a coordination, 'although' a concession, etc. They can also find it helpful to locate the beginning and the end of the main clause, or the subject(s) and verb(s) of the clauses of a sentence, and so on.

It is my impression that most teachers spend more time on translations from Danish into English than the other way round. Again, no translation theory is taught for the translation of Danish passages into English, but I have found it very profitable to gather some seemingly disconnected phenomena into ordered clusters: thus, the difference between teach/learn, take/bring, lend/borrow, go (or get)/come, wave/beckon, sell/buy is mainly one of direction: is the movement towards, or away from, the speaker or the centre of interest? By the same token, a considerable number of Danish prepositional groups can be lumped together as instances of the objective genitive, in which case the English preposition is 'of' (the murder of the king, the explanation of the problem, etc.).

Collecting linguistic phenomena into clusters of the kind just outlined has the great pedagogic advantage that the pupils have to burden their brains with fewer isolated instances: generalizations have always proved far easier to cope with.

And remarkable things come to pass: the more the pupil advances, the more he will know where the shoe pinches. And the more he comes to look upon language as an object to be analysed, the more individual rules and exceptions will be seen as parts of an even larger pattern which the teaching may make him more and more anxious to examine.

6. Aims and Results

What is the ideal for a Grammar School translation, be it into or from the mother tongue? The spontaneous reply would be 'one that gets the meaning across without being necessarily a verbatim rendering of the original'.

Few people would probably object to that criterion. But surely, the tone is of some importance, too? A witty original should not be transformed into a boring exercise, and if irony is a characteristic of the material to be translated, it should certainly be perceptible in the translated end product as well.

A good question to ask when evaluating a pupil's oral or written performance would seem to be the following one: what does the oral or written message communicate, and to what extent is it likely to be accepted by a native speaker?

Of course it is desirable for a translation into English to be good not only in terms of translation (i.e. so as not to offend a native speaker and to be reasonably faithful to the original), but also as a specimen of English prose. In the early stages of Grammar School teaching, that is only a minor problem because, as was pointed out earlier, the Danish translation pieces are adapted in such a way as to be susceptible of verbatim transference. But later, when translation texts leave more options open, translation competence comes to form a major dividing line in the classroom: the weaker sort of pupil, leaning heavily on the Danish original, does produce a translation, but the result is not very fluent or elegant English. However, by that time, the more competent pupils will be able to acquit themselves quite creditably within the field of idiomatic rendition.

How free should a translation be allowed to be? No hard-and-fast rules can be given, but it would seem to be better for a translation not to worry too much about word-to-word correspondences and to make sense in English of the Danish message, than for a translation to follow the Danish version slavishly and unimaginatively - and produce miserable English.

Of course a considerable knowledge of English is required if a Grammar School pupil is to be able to write acceptable English without being unfair to the Danish prototype. The point is that, even at Grammar School level, translation does not have to be sheer mechanical routine. As mentioned earlier, a translation will fail miserably if the translator does not understand the original version down to the smallest detail. Translation thus instils in pupils a respect for texts and a sensitivity to the ways they are structured. It makes them more careful, and probably also better, readers because their understanding of a text comes to include familiarity with its nuances and awareness of its undertones.

It is probably superfluous to observe that translations into Danish of English literary masterpieces do not become works of art in their own right. We do not use Danish blank verse for the Shakespearean metre, one reason being that in Danish literature blank verse is not surrounded with a prestige at all comparable to the aura of the English blank verse. Nor do we render lyrical poetry by Danish rhymed lines, etc. In such cases, it would be more correct to talk about groping and tentative approximations than translations. However, where modern prose texts are concerned, such as, for example, newspaper articles, it is often possible to achieve a fairly precise rendering, not only of the content, but also of the tone and the style of the English version.

It is vital to instil a feeling of respect for precision into the pupils as they advance in their knowledge of the foreign language. Precision of presentation is indispensable in most communication situations, also in such as are not unduly specialized or professional. That is why errors like those mentioned in 3.4. (Transference from Danish) above should of course be corrected. If the message is not reasonably exact, more than the wording will suffer: the sender's personality may tend to appear in a more or less distorted light - he may e.g. seem wishy-washy, immature, or nervous if his English message does not have some measure of idiomatic pithiness.

Also, it is of crucial importance to translate whole passages as well as individual words or shorter paragraphs: translation is eminently a syntactic discipline, which may provide pupils with 'idiomatic bundles' to be exploited and elaborated at their discretion.

Finally, a by no means negligible side-effect of regular translation exercises is that pupils' eyes will be opened to the fact that there are different types of error, and that some errors are worse than others. The touchstone is a native speaker's imagined reaction.

7. Conclusion

The present article has limited itself to dealing with the teaching of English in Danish Grammar Schools. Some of the questions that immediately present themselves when the topic is translation have been discussed. A few of them have been tentatively answered, but others have been left as questions, either because they are inherently unanswerable or because any answer given will depend on the personality and pedagogic ideology of the person who attempts to offer an answer.

The difficulty that many Danes face when learning English is that a good many Danish patterns can be immediately transferred into English, whereas others emphatically cannot. Translation may be instrumental in opening pupils' eyes to 'false friends' as well as true ones, and may simply encourage them to show some degree of attention before they plunge headlong: when is a verbatim rendering possible or even preferable, and when is freedom necessary?

Only spies need a linguistic (and behavioural!) competence enabling them to fit unobtrusively into an English setting. What Grammar School pupils need to learn is not to make fools of themselves the moment they open their mouths to speak English.

The usefulness, indeed indispensability, of translation where contrastive analysis is concerned, is beyond question. It is true that in the classroom such analyses assume modest proportions, mainly concentrating on selected individual items, such as different conceptual areas covered by the Danish *træ* and *skov* and the English 'tree', 'wood', and 'forest'. Or the different treatments given to adjectives used as substantives in the two languages. As was pointed out earlier, such problems may of course be discussed and explained in English, but occasional translation is not only a time-saver, it is also, for some pupils, a shortcut to understanding. Besides, errors of translation may in such cases serve a useful function because they show the teacher how to gear his teaching to his pupils' needs.

Translation is sometimes associated with 'traditional', not to say old-fashioned methods of teaching. Of course the ultimate aim for Grammar School pupils is to achieve a by no means negligible competence in English, for which reason a lot of English should be spoken (and read) in class. And, equally evidently, translation should not determine the teaching or in any other way be an obstacle to the pupils' language acquisition.

What is needed in the discussion about the pros and cons of translation is not acrimonious intransigence, but rather exchanges of balanced and well-argued views. The question should be discussed without fanaticism, and the angle of approach should be pedagogic expediency rather than methodological purity.

Intelligent pupils will benefit from any decent kind of teaching, no matter what method is adopted. But classroom activities are not meant for the top five per cent only, and it is an empirical fact that, to the majority of Grammar School pupils, translation is a serviceable means to an end, viz. language acquisition. One need only refer to the innumerable cases when the teacher bombards his pupils and is, in turn, bombarded by them, with questions like, 'What is the Danish equivalent for that word?' or 'How can that idea be rendered in English?'

Translation is not a panacea, but it certainly covers some of the requirements of the learner as well as the teacher. It would be absurd to spurn such a useful ingredient of the teaching.

Notes

1.   Although it is only a partial equivalent, Grammar School has been used throughout the article to refer to the Danish *gymnasium*, as this is the rendering most frequently encountered.

Translation as a Unifying Discipline

Knud Sørensen

1. Introduction

In course of time many doubts have been voiced about the relevance of translation to the study of foreign languages. Admittedly, it is one of the essential aims of the advanced student of a foreign language to develop an ability to detach himself from his native language and to learn to receive and convey messages exclusively in the foreign language. It is, however, also extremely valuable for the student to contrast the two languages he is concerned with, by developing skills in translating from his native language into the foreign language and vice versa. The following pages are intended as a plea for translation as a highly useful discipline, in the exercise of which the student should utilize the knowledge he has acquired through the study of other important disciplines.

When he is confronted with a text for translation, the student is first of all forced to study it with concentration - something akin to the close-reading technique that he is familiar with from his study of literature. The point is, of course, that he has to do with a *text*, and a text has certain characteristics: it is normally consistent and coherent. What this means is, among other things, that if in his study of the text the translator comes across a word or an expression that does not appear to make sense, he can be pretty sure that in most cases it is he himself who has failed to grasp the writer's intention and that it is not the writer who is at fault. Naturally, such seeming 'oddities' are particularly frequent if the text the translator has in front of him is in the foreign language; his incomprehension may then be due to either ignorance about a linguistic point or to his inability to follow the argument of the text, or to a combination of both. It is more striking that the translator may also occasionally come across such 'oddities' when he studies a text in his native language. This should be an eye-opener, leading to the realization that one does not fully 'know' one's native language, and that is a salutary experience.

Essentially, the translator's task consists in rendering the full import of a given text into another language in such a way that the result is idiomatic (it should not read like a translation) and conforms stylistically to the original. This is the goal to be striven for; but there is no cause for despair if that goal is sometimes unattainable. From a realistic point of view it is as well to admit that occasionally the translator has to be content with undertranslation, overtranslation, or paraphrase. In most cases, however, the goal - or at least a close approximation to it - *is* attainable, provided the translator is suitably equipped.

What are the requirements to be met by a competent translator? Besides possessing a well-developed awareness of the characteristics of his native language, he should have near-native proficiency in the foreign language, including a thorough knowledge of its cultural and social fabric. He should bring to the task of translation the knowledge and experience he has acquired in his study of grammar, literature, history, and civics. He should of course also be able and willing to treat loyally and faithfully any text with whose contents he may not personally sympathize.

2. Interference

After these general remarks let us now approach the actual task, examining some examples of the dangers and difficulties that confront the translator.

Where the two languages involved are English and Danish, it is perhaps natural to assume that similarities outweigh differences. It is for instance a fact that in most cases representatives of the different word-classes correspond in the two languages, though this is not invariably so; and similarly, there is frequent syntactic conformity between English and Danish, but here again there are exceptions. Where the two languages do not conform, there is a danger of interference. A Dane translating a text from Danish into English may be tempted to perpetrate Danicisms, and if he translates from English into Danish he may inadvertently introduce Anglicisms. A good illustration of interference is the way dependent interrogative clauses, whether English or Danish, are sometimes handled by translators.

Questions in which the subject is a *wh-* pronoun have the same structure in English independent and dependent clauses:

Who did it? I don't know who did it.

Danish on the other hand, uses different structures:

Hvem gjorde det? Jeg ved ikke, hvem der gjorde det.

Danish dependent interrogative clauses require the presence of 'formal situative *der*'[1] after *hv-* words that are (part of) the subject.

Now it may be noted that Danish journalists and others, who write with English-language texts at their elbows, are sometimes tempted to leave out this *der*, presumably because it has no equivalent in English:

En opdeling af, hvilken type sygeplejersker var rygere, gav dette resultat ...

Ligesom dengang summer magtens korridorer med spørgsmålene om, hvem i Det Hvide Hus vidste besked ...

Such examples contain Anglicisms; and there are parallel examples of Danicisms to be found. When Danes translate dependent interrogative clauses into English, they may be tempted to introduce a *who* (which often corresponds to relative *der*, but of course not to situative *der*), the result being an unEnglish construction. The example that follows (from an examination paper) is typical:

Det er mere end bittert at konstatere, hvor mange mennesker der lader hånt om advarsler.

This was translated as follows:

It is more than bitter to find how many people who disregard warnings.

After this exemplification of interference we may now proceed to a discussion of some problem areas that confront the translator who translates from Danish into English.

3. Adverbial vs. Adjectival Constructions

As mentioned, there is normally word-class equivalence between the two languages, so that adjective corresponds to adjective, adverb to adverb, etc. It should be noted, however, that in some cases where Danish makes use of an adverbial construction, English would typically prefer an adjectival construction, so that *Han tog aktivt del i arbejdet* corresponds to 'He took an active part in the work'. Similarly, *Der skete af og til afbrydelser* corresponds to 'There were occasional interruptions' (though an adverbial construction is possible, but less frequent). In some cases there are both possibilities in both languages, Danish preferring an adverb, English an adjective: *Han kom tidligt på foråret / i det tidlige forår*: 'He came in the early spring / early in the spring'. In other cases the distribution seems to be that Danish only allows an adverbial construction while English has two possibilities: *blot 60.000 vælgere*: 'a mere 60,000 voters' ('just', 'merely'); *tilsyneladende uden grund*: 'for no apparent reason' ('apparently'); *Den mand, der kom ind, var åbenbart tysker*: 'The man who entered was an obvious German' ('obviously'). Occasionally one may note another type of word-class inconformity: some Danish adverbs are most idiomatically rendered by verbs whose semantic make-up accommodates the relevant adverbial element: *den stemning, som fortsat præger landet*: 'the atmosphere that continues to characterize the country'; *meget, der tidligere var tabubelagt*: 'many things that used to be taboo'; *problemet er stadig uløst*: 'the problem remains unsolved'.

4. Sentence vs. Non-Sentence

English has greater scope than Danish for nominal constructions without finite verbs. In an example like *Det var en maskine, han selv havde opfundet* we have a construction with two clauses containing finite verbs, which could easily be translated verbatim: 'It was an engine he had himself invented'. But clause does not necessarily correspond to clause, and the Danish example could also be rendered 'It was an engine of his own invention', so that a Danish clause may be the equivalent of an English nominal construction. In an example like *citater, som man kan tvivle på kommer sagen ved* we have the natural Danish formulation, with *citater af tvivlsom relevans* as a rather formal alternative; the natural English translation of this is 'quotations of doubtful relevance'. Similar examples are: *Han fremhævede, hvor vigtigt det var, at han modtog svar hurtigt*: 'He stressed the importance of an early reply'; *Vi lægger stor vægt på, at disse regler nøje overholdes*: 'We attach great importance to a strict observance of these rules'.

5. Indications of Time

The following quotation, *De sidste år har afsløret, at der findes meget forskellige holdninger til flygtninge* represents a minority construction; for in Danish, points of time or periods of time are normally manifested in the form of adverbials (*i de sidste år*). On the other hand it is very common for English to have indications of time in the subject slot, the verbs forming part of this construction being chiefly 'find' and 'see': 'Christmas morning found her bustling in the kitchen'; 'A day or two should see the end of our troubles'; 'The next second confirmed my suspicion'. This construction may even occur where a temporal element is merely implied: 'The low turnout by voters in France's cantonal elections has overshadowed the result which saw the Socialist party making a net gain of 89 seats'. It should be added, however, that it is always possible for English to convey temporal notions in the form of adverbials. In this area we have a typical situation: in Danish there is a dominant adverbial construction with subject function for time indications being marginally possible, while English has two constructions that are perhaps equally frequent and certainly equally acceptable. Translating an English construction in which a time indication is the subject into Danish hardly presents a problem; but when the translator translates from Danish into English, it is useful for him to bear in mind the asymmetrical relationship holding in this area, and it makes for stylistic variation if he exploits both possibilities in English.

6. Danish *med* and English 'with'

These two prepositions correspond in many cases. But Danes tend to overgeneralize, assuming a correspondence also when translating sequences where *med* collocates for instance with an adjective in examples of the type *Det er godt / interessant / nødvendigt / relevant / usandsynligt med et samarbejde*: 'It is good, etc. to have co-operation'. But in this case the prepositions are not equivalent, and the point is elusive because there is only negative evidence available: a corresponding construction does not exist in English.

7. Irreversible Binominals

Both English and Danish have a number of cliché-like co-ordinate pairs, irreversible binominals, some of which appear in parallel form in the two languages: *død og ødelæggelse*: 'death and destruction'; *eder og forbandelser*: 'oaths and imprecations'; *udbud og efterspørgsel*: 'supply and demand'. But in many others the ordering of the items is different in the two languages. The translator should be on his guard here, remembering that *frem og tilbage* corresponds to 'backwards and forwards' (or 'back and forth'), *ud og ind* to 'in and out', *kvit eller dobbelt* to 'double or quits', *vand og brød* to 'bread and water', *mål og vægt* to 'weights and measures', and *et had-kærlighedsforhold* to 'a love-hate relationship'. Danish normally has *salt og peber*, while English has both 'salt and pepper' (condiments) and 'pepper and salt' (colour).[2]

8. *Les faux amis*

English and Danish share a number of Romance loanwords having identical or similar forms; some of them have the same meaning in the two languages (for instance *pueril*: 'puerile', *senil*: 'senile'), but others do not agree in meaning. Thus Danish *frivol* means 'indelicate', 'improper', while English 'frivolous' approaches the meaning 'silly', as in 'a frivolous remark'. Further examples of these semantic will-o'-the-wisps are *chikane* ('pinpricks') vs. 'chicane(ry)' (trickery); *eventuelt*: ('possibly') vs. 'eventually' (at long last); *fundament* ('foundation') vs. 'fundament' (the buttocks); *genial* ('of genius') vs. 'genial' (cheerful, warm); and *triviel* ('tedious, commonplace') vs. 'trivial' (slight, unimportant). A sub-group is made up of pseudo-English words in Danish: their form is English, but they do not mean in English what they mean in Danish. Examples of these are Danish *butterfly*: 'bow-tie', *sixpence*: 'cloth cap', *speaker*: 'announcer', *speeder*: 'accelerator', and *struggler:* 'social climber'.

9. Political Terminology

This presents special problems. In the first place the translator sometimes has to operate with three sets of terms, depending on whether he has to cope with texts describing conditions in (1) Britain, (2) the United States, or (3) the rest of the world. Thus, *udenrigsministeren* is (1) the Foreign Secretary, (2) the Secretary of State, or (3) the Foreign Minister, and the department he is responsible for is (1) the Foreign Office, (2) the State Department, or (3) the Ministry of Foreign (or External) Affairs. (If politicians from several countries are referred to in the same context, the compromise solution may be as follows: 'the foreign ministers of the United States, China, the Soviet Union, France and Britain'). Similarly, *finansministeren* is (1) the Chancellor (of the Exchequer), (2) the Secretary of the Treasury, or (3) the Minister of Finance. *Generalsekretær* is normally secretary-general, for instance the Secretary-General of the United Nations, but we speak of the Soviet General Secretary (Mikhail Gorbachev).

In the second place the fact must be faced that there may be a mismatch between the institutions of different countries. For instance, the functions performed by the Danish Minister of Justice are shared in Britain by the Home Secretary and the Lord Chancellor (among others). Such titles are therefore strictly speaking untranslatable. Dictionaries will provide some help as to political terminology, and besides, one can turn to works like *Britain - An Official Handbook* and *The World Almanac and Book of Facts,* both of which appear annually.

The points discussed so far are probably most important to bear in mind when one translates from Danish into English. Let us now consider some points that are relevant to translation from English into Danish.

10. Anaphora vs. Cataphora

As far as the use of anaphoric (back-referring) and cataphoric (forward-referring) personal pronouns is concerned, the two languages have the same patterns, but the distribution of the patterns differs. In English, anaphora (a) and cataphora (b) are equally acceptable:

(a) When *John* came home, *he* had a beer.
(b) When *he* came home, *John* had a beer.

(It is assumed that there is coreference between name and pronoun). In Danish, the (a) construction is the preferred one in probably 19 cases out of 20, while the (b) construction is the marked pattern. This being the case, it is advisable for the translator to turn any (b) construction that he comes across in English into an (a) construction in his Danish version; if not, he runs the risk that his translation will produce a slightly odd effect. A marked construction should normally be avoided unless it corresponds to a marked construction in the original.

11. Premodification

Contemporary English often makes use of heavy premodification, for instance in the form of so-called string compounds: 'a strong, I'm-the-guy-in-charge-now voice'. Since Danish has much more limited scope for premodification, it would be unidiomatic to transfer such a construction unchanged into Danish. Instead, a combination of pre-and postmodification may be used: *en kraftig stemme, der udtrykte ...*

12. Lexical Anglicisms

After these syntactic points we may next consider some lexical problems. Foremost among them is perhaps the problem of Anglicisms. At present, Danish is being exposed to a torrent of English words and phrases, particularly in the media, which often draw on English-language sources. There are different types of loans, among them direct loans (*yuppie*), loan translations (*kropssprog*, from 'body language'), semantic loans (*en snæver sejr*, from 'a **narrow** victory'), and idioms (*holde en lav profil*, from 'keep a low profile'). The examples just given are frequent in contemporary Danish usage, and once such loans have become fully established, it does not make much sense trying to oust them. But where the loans are not fully established and appear to be superfluous, the translator should try to stem the tide. Thus 'the Reagan Administration' should be rendered *Reagan-regeringen* rather than *Reagan-administrationen*, 'network' should become *net* rather than *netværk*, and in an example like 'The party gained nine seats', *mandater* rather than *sæder* should be used.

A special problem arises where English has a word that appears in two senses while the corresponding, often formally similar, Danish word is used in one sense only. A case in point is 'frustrate': *frustrere*. In suitable contexts the two words may be equated, for instance 'The lack of money frustrated him': *... frustrerede ham*, where the verbs refer to feelings. But the English verb can also mean 'prevent (the fulfilment of a plan)' as in 'They succeeded in frustrating the enemy in his plans', and here it corresponds to Danish *forhindre*.

In such cases a scrutiny of context and collocation is crucial and may often help the translator to arrive at the correct solution. The English adjective 'national' may approach the meaning of 'patriotic', as in 'National passions have been raised', and in such a collocation it corresponds to Danish *national*; but where the English adjective means 'relating to a whole country', as in 'on a national basis' or 'a national newspaper', the Danish equivalents are *lands-* or *landsdækkende.* Compare further 'the original inhabitants' (first) and 'an original thinker' (not imitative); 'There is no cause for concern - the storm was not too serious', where 'concern' means 'worry', and 'Education in the 12 Inner London Boroughs is the concern of the ILEA', where 'concern' is synonymous with 'responsibility'.

13. Differing Specification

Examining the context is also important if the members of corresponding semantic fields in the two languages belong to different levels of abstraction. For instance, some English words are less specific than their nearest Danish equivalents. A 'mount' is any animal that one rides (*ridedyr,* a word that is not much used), and a suitable context is required for the translator to decide whether the animal involved is a horse, a donkey, an elephant, etc. A 'charge' can mean 'anybody one is responsible for'; there is no single Danish term that covers it, and depending on the context, one's charge may denote, say, a baby, a prisoner, or a halfwit. Again, out of context it is impossible to determine the precise implications of 'foul play', an expression that ranges semantically from 'skulduggery' to 'murder'. Correspondingly, there are some Danish words that lack specification in comparison with English. For instance, *nedbør* is an umbrella term that covers rain, snow, and hail; it is true that there exists the English term 'precipitation' in a corresponding sense, but that word has a limited register, being a technical meteorological term. Depending on circumstances, the noun in *de har håndværkere* may refer to joiners, painters, plumbers, etc. And *en rund fødselsdag* may refer to any of a number of birthdays on which a round number is reached; that number would be specified in English. In such cases the two languages differ as far as the degree of semantic specification is concerned.

Another difference may be that where Danish has a colourful term, English only possesses a rather pale equivalent; compare *sofavælger:* 'abstainer' (at an election) and *kolumbusæg:* 'an unexpectedly simple solution'. Or it may be the other way round. In an example like 'Bad weather put paid to his chances of winning', the vivid verbal phrase can only be rendered by the rather pale *gjorde ende på.*

Idioms, metaphors, and proverbs present special problems. It is true that they are sometimes very close to each other in the two languages: *male fanden på væggen:* 'paint the devil on the wall'; *leve fra hånden og i munden:* 'live from hand to mouth'. In other cases, however, they differ to a greater or lesser degree. English has 'the goose that lays the golden eggs', while in Danish it is the hen that does it. While in English 'the ostrich buries its head in the sand', its Danish opposite number *stikker hovedet i busken*. Some English idioms and proverbs are frequently misunderstood by Danes. Thus, 'to live like fighting cocks' means 'to have lots of good food', not 'to lead a cat-and-dog life', and the proverb 'One man's meat is another man's poison' corresponds to Danish *Hvad der kurerer en smed, slår en skrædder ihjel*, not to *Den enes død er den andens brød*, which latter saying can only be conveyed through a pale English paraphrase: 'One man's loss is another man's gain'. The last example typifies one kind of incongruity: the Danish saying is colourful, while the nearest English equivalent is pale. A further example of this type is: *Som man råber i skoven, får man svar*, which can be paraphrased 'If one makes rude remarks, one must expect a rude reply'. But sometimes it is the other way round: English has a colourful saying, Danish a pale one. This may be exemplified by the proverb 'You cannot make a silk purse out of a sow's ear', in the rendering of which Danish has to resort to a paraphrase (*Man kan ikke frembringe et godt resultat, hvis ens materiale er dårligt*); the saying *at lave en silkepung af et svineøre*, recorded in *Ordbog over det danske sprog*, is practically obsolete today.

14. Quotation and Allusion

It is a decided advantage for the translator to be well read in classical English literature since many American and British writers have the habit of interlarding their writing with literary allusions. If this is done in the form of a regular quotation, it is usually not too difficult to trace it even though a quotation may only ring a vague bell; one can consult a dictionary of quotations. For adequate translation it is often important to examine a quotation in its context. If, for instance, a Biblical quotation is involved (it will usually be from the King James Bible of 1611), it will be necessary to locate the corresponding passage of the Danish translation of the Bible. In *Major Barbara* Bernard Shaw has one of his characters say: 'I'm none of your common hewers of wood and drawers of water ...' (Penguin edition 1945, p. 71); this comes from Joshua 9. 21: 'let them be hewers of wood and drawers of water', which corresponds to the Danish Bible translation: '*de skal ... være brændehuggere og vandbærere ...*'. In the example that follows:

It was mad-dogs-and-Englishmen weather in Washington and, although the air conditioners whirred throughout the city, everyone left who could. (*Time* 18.08.1975, p. 24) one can form a rough idea of the kind of weather referred to even if the hidden quotation remains hidden. But the journalist must have assumed that his readers were familiar with Noel Coward's poem Mad Dogs and Englishmen:

> Mad dogs and Englishmen go out in the mid-day sun;
> The Japanese don't care to, the Chinese wouldn't dare to;
> Hindus and Argentines sleep firmly from twelve to one,
> But Englishmen detest a siesta.

Writers frequently take liberties with their sources, and unless one is well read, it can be difficult to make sense of the garbled version of a quotation and trace it to its source, and this is often necessary if one is to understand it fully. Here are a handful of such garbled quotations, with their sources appended:

> Football returns, with its court of juvenile rioters (a season of fists and callow bootfulness) ... (*The Listener* 11.9.1975, p. 324; cf. John Keats, *To Autumn*: 'Season of mists and mellow fruitfulness ...')

> [an American] ... standing amid the alien porn of Soho, six thousand miles from home ... (David Lodge, *Changing Places*, London 1975, p.96; cf. John Keats, *Ode to a Nightingale*: 'She stood in tears amid the alien corn ...')

> He did not despise learning, only those who forgot that a little, combined with a lot of self-satisfaction, could be a very dangerous thing in the last quarter of this tormented century. (*The Listener* 20.11.1975, p. 671; cf. Alexander Pope, *An Essay on Criticism*: 'A little learning is a dang'rous thing ...')

> Not allowed to reason why, he could only do and die as gracefully as possible. (*The Listener* 20.11.1975, p. 694; cf. Alfred Tennyson, *The Charge of the Light Brigade*: 'Their's not to make reply, / Their's not to reason why, / Their's but to do and die ...')

> Both the new plays last week were comedies, for which much thanks. (*The Listener* 27.1.1977, p. 119; cf. Shakespeare, *Hamlet*, 1.1.8: 'For this relief much thanks ...')

A knowledge of proverbs may also be essential, as appears from the following example:

> ... a modest bomb explosion in the Festival's Palace, which left the local gendarmerie excitedly bolting stable doors and searching ladies' hand-bags ... (*The Listener* 29.5.1975, p.714; cf. the proverb 'It is too late to bolt the stable-door after the horse has escaped').

15. Conclusion

In the preceding pages it has been my endeavour to show that translation is not just a narrowly linguistic operation; for translation to succeed, the translator must not only develop an acute awareness of the similarities and differences between the two languages he is concerned with, he must also be thoroughly imbued with literature and culture, the latter term being understood in a wide sense. Coping with texts for translation necessitates the mobilization of knowledge from all important areas of the socio-cultural structure that language reflects. It is in this sense that translation becomes a unifying discipline.

Notes

1. Paul Diderichsen, *Elementær Dansk Grammatik*, second edition, Copenhagen 1957, p. 183.
2. D.A. Cruse, *Lexical Semantics*. Cambridge Textbooks in Linguistics, Cambridge University Press 1986, p. 47.

Information Processing in Translation and some Pedagogic Perspectives

Margrethe Mondahl & Knud Anker Jensen

ABSTRACT

The paper will comment on advanced learners' processing of linguistic knowledge in connection with a translation task from Danish into English. We shall focus on learners' use of different types of linguistic knowledge, on the degree to which they use it and on the form in which it is represented. The following issues will be taken up: *introspection*[1] as an elicitation method in data collection, a *theoretical model* based on cognitive psychology, a taxonomy of three types of *knowledge representation* and an analysis of *learners' mental representations of linguistic knowledge* along two dimensions. Finally we shall discuss some pedagogic perspectives of the findings - in particular the role of *grammar instruction* in the classroom.

The analysis shows that if the learner does not identify any particular problems, solutions are based on *skill- and rule-based knowledge*. If the learner identifies problems, the solution pattern is one that should involve the application of *knowledge- or rule-based knowledge*. The linguistically most competent learners in the present corpus are able to activate skill- or, as a maximum, rule-based knowledge.

1. Introduction

The following is an analysis of Danish learners' solutions to the task: *a translation from Danish into English*. Focus is on the types of knowledge used by the informants, the degree to which they have access to knowledge, and the form this knowledge takes. The first section describes the informants' educational backgrounds. The second section outlines our method of data collection: *introspection*; this is followed by a brief comment on the advantages and disadvantages of using this form of elicitation. The third section describes in more detail how the method was used in practice in video recordings. The central section is the theoretical section, which outlines our categories of analysis; these are based on models of *cognitive psychology* and *artificial 'intelligent' systems*. The section on theory is concluded by a model of the development of *ideal translation competence*. Following this, we include our informants' task solutions and an outline is given of the conventions used in protocol transcripts. After this, extracts from informant introspection are presented together with an analysis of their information processing. The analysis is based on our cognitive model, outlined below. The informants are rated both relative to each other and in relation to the outline of ideal translation competence. On the basis of the results of our analysis, we finally discuss *pedagogic perspectives*, in particular the role of *grammar instruction*.

2. Informants

We have two groups of informants whose instructional focuses are different: Group 1 from The Copenhagen Business School and Group 2 from the Danish Civil Defence Corps Academy.

The Group 1 informants are studying English at university level; the aim of their education is to make them professional translators and interpreters, especially with regard to the translation of ESP texts. It is considered important for the candidates to reach a *high level of linguistic competence* and to be acquainted with *scientific methods* which will enable them to carry out investigations into the use of ESP, do research, and teach at university level. Translation and grammar are the subjects studied that we are interested in here. Within these subjects, instruction is aimed at enabling the students to: 'produce linguistically correct, adequate and stylistically correct translations into and from the L2' and 'increase theoretical and practical grammatical knowledge', and produce 'a well-argumented and systematic account of grammatical rules and relations' (*Studievejledning EK/EOT*, 1985, Copenhagen Business School, our translation).

The Group 2 informants' education aims at enabling the students (who will be commissioned officers at the end of their 4-year course) to function as leaders at intermediate level, i.e. be responsible for the planning of instruction for conscripted personnel and NCOs, lead and command a force of about 100 men, and perform administrative and other duties in connection with international cooperation. On top of civil defence subjects and leadership instruction, these informants' education has a general part which includes German and English. The English course takes up 150 hours and focuses on: 'enabling the student to prepare and carry out instruction in English and participate in meetings at which English is used' (*Bestemmelser for uddannelsen, Videregående Befalingsmands uddannelse*, 1987, our translation).

The two groups of informants distinguish themselves by having different instructional foci, and it is our assumption that this will be reflected in their information processing, in their approach to the task, and in their ability to verbalise about linguistic problems in relation to the task set.

3. Method

In our investigation we use *introspection* to elicit information about the information processing of the study's informants. This method is based on a range of assumptions which we shall present below.

Introspective methods have been the subject of much debate. The methods were first used by psychologists to investigate human problem-solving strategies; as we consider the processing of linguistic material and the production of language as problem solving, the method is well suited for eliciting data about the information processing involved in the solution of a translation task. Using introspective methods is not unproblematic, however; the method has been criticised for:

- not giving access to all processes,
- only revealing the product and not the process,
- changing information processing as a result of the demand for verbalisation,
- revealing only part of the information processing.

We shall not deal with this criticism here, but we refer the reader to Nisbett and Wilson (1977) and Boersch (1986) for detailed discussion. We are of the opinion that despite the points of criticism mentioned above, our cognitive model (see below) warrants the use of introspective methods.

Two methods of introspection are used. They are both assumed to provide information about the processing related to the task set; they are: *loud-thinking* and *retrospection*. Loud-thinking is characterised by being verbalisation that is simultaneous with task solution; it elicits information on the informant's use of *automised* or *controlled* processes by being the direct coding of the conscious thought and by eliciting information about the content of *short term memory* at a given point in time (see the section on The Cognitive Model for a more detailed discussion of this).

In this study we are primarily interested in the information rendered by loud-thinking on the question of whether an informant has automised a process or not. If there is loud-thinking on an issue the process can be described as more or less controlled, if no loud-thinking is found, the process has been automised (see section on Analysis for examples of this).

In the retrospection we find data that are collected by the researcher immediately after task completion. The retrospection is carried out in the following way. There has to be contextual information - in this case the informant's translation together with extracts from the video-recording, which show how the informant acted in the situation in question. The researcher does not discuss matters that do not relate directly to the task set, as this might give an incorrect picture of the information processing involved. The retrospection is an elaboration of what the informant did during loud-thinking. It is an important part of data collection as it may provide more information and lead to further comments which can be central to the interpretation of the informant's information processing.

The researcher gets the opportunity to ask further questions and focus on subjects that are of special interest. In the present study interest centred around the informants' use of analysed knowledge and their use of the control dimension. We assume that the loud-thinking will primarily elicit information about the control dimension whereas the retrospection session will primarily elicit information on the informant's use of analysed knowledge.

4. Design

The data used in the study were collected in the following way. A number of informants were selected: five in each group. They were asked to complete the same translation task. The task had been selected with a view to providing as much information as possible about the informants' information processing in relation to the expression of future reference in English. The informants had no access to reference books or grammars while solving the task. After the informant had produced the translation *per se* and thought aloud in connection with this, the retrospection session was carried out. The informant had not been informed about this in advance. In the retrospection session, the translation - which had been written on a vufoil - and/or the video-recording of task solution were used to support the informant's memory. After the completion of the test, the tapes were transcribed and qualitative analyses of the protocols were made.

After a preliminary analysis of the transcripts, four informants - two from each group - were selected for further analysis. These informants illustrate characteristic information processing. The analyses are based on a simple system of categories; the reasons for using this system and an outline of it is given below.

5.0 The Cognitive Model

The aim of this section is to give a brief description of the theoretical framework on which we base the categories of analysis. It should be stressed that as is the case with all models, this one is also a simplification of reality.

The starting point is that using a language is a *complex skill* which can be analysed at several levels. We are particularly interested in the types of linguistic knowledge that contribute to the production of translations. Knowledge is used in its broadest sense: it refers to the total mental activity behind any linguistic action, that is, both conscious knowledge that the informant can verbalise about and knowledge to which there is not direct access.

5.1 Learning

We consider learning as the development of new programmes which can process and produce data. The basic difference between man and machine is - from this point of view - that man is *self-programming*, because he is equipped with intentions and acts within contexts where his actions are important in the form of reactions to the changing demands of the surrounding world.

How do we learn then? First in a purely quantitative way by the addition of knowledge. But taking in new knowledge is always dependent on already existing knowledge; at the same time it restructures already existing knowledge (Piaget's assimilation and accommodation). Self-programming is therefore dependent on the present status of the system, input from the surrounding world and feedback on its own product; it may consist of knowledge extension, restructuring or more effective access to existing knowledge (see also sections on Analysis and Control). This leads to a description of how knowledge is stored in memory.

5.2 The Structure of Knowledge

Our model of mental knowledge representation has two elements: a knowledge base, and the procedures which interpret and manipulate this base. There is no universally correct model of the mental representation of knowledge, but a general framework can be set up on the basis of what memory should be able to provide:

1. registration of events and an evaluation of whether storage is worthwhile;
2. the establishment of a mental representation of an event in memory;
3. potential long time storage of the event in memory;
4. the rapid and efficient retrieval from memory when necessary, either controlled or automatic (see below);
5. conscious storage of retrieved information for a brief period during which it contributes to thought.

(Johnson-Laird 1988:143).

This provides a division into three components: a *short term memory* in which incoming data and retrieved knowledge are stored briefly under the subject's attention while they are part of ongoing thinking; a *long term memory* in which data have been stored as traces in memory that can be activated in a given situation; and a *control unit* which regulates the system.

After being processed in the perceptual system, incoming data meet data from long-term memory. The elements of short-term memory that are under conscious control are termed *working memory*. This is where thinking *per se* takes place.

Long-term memory is divided into two types of knowledge: a permanent memory for important skills - *procedural knowledge* - and a memory which comprises former experiences and factual knowledge - *declarative knowledge.*

Declarative knowledge is *analytic* and this is where we find analysed rule systems. This is the type of knowledge that the informant has most direct access to and which he can account for most thoroughly.

However, only part of thinking is controlled by conscious rules. A large part of the mental activity takes place in unanalysed knowledge structures. An unanalysed knowledge structure is not an unsystematic structure, but a structure to which the individual does not have direct access. Procedural knowledge is more *holistic* than declarative knowledge.

The two categories of knowledge are not sharply distinguished types of knowledge but rather a continuum of knowledge, and knowledge may be more or less analysed. In relation to language this is found in the difference between the exhaustive grammatical explanation and the non-exhaustive rule of thumb.

Anderson proposes the following model for knowledge representation called ACT*:

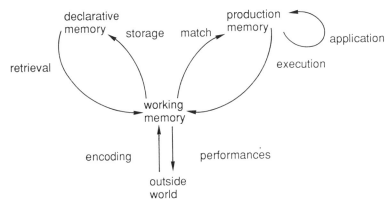

Figure 1

ACT* is a theory of cognitive architecture - that is, a theory of the basic principles of operation built into the cognitive system. ACT stands for Adaptive Control of Thought (Anderson 1983: 19 and ix).

5.3 Use of Knowledge: Production

We are now able to describe the relationship between declarative and procedural knowledge and their activation in task completion. Anderson (1985) views the acquisition of a skill as three-phased. In the first, cognitive phase, the skill is carried out by means of the rules of explicit, declarative knowledge (knowledge-based knowledge: know-why). In the second phase *compiling* of information processing takes place. A simplified explanation is that this involves a restructuring of knowledge representation where informed conclusions are drawn by the subject (rule-based knowledge: know-how). In the last phase the result is brought about via a pattern which is activated without the introduction of conscious rule knowledge (skill-based knowledge: know-when).

Rasmussen (1985) operates on the basis of the same three stage model, but the relationship between declarative and procedural knowledge is analysed differently. Procedural knowledge is not compiled declarative knowledge, but a fundamentally different knowledge representation, which

75

is established via practice under the governing control of analysed knowledge.

In the initial phases, the skill in question is carried out under attentional control, but later the new knowledge is disconnected from rule-based knowledge and it becomes a new type of knowledge, which has its own regularities. The new type of knowledge is holistic and is triggered through signs in the incoming data ('encoding'). Simultaneously, conscious knowledge of the more abstract rules, which the activity was originally based on, may disappear. (Rasmussen 1987:18).

5.4 Access to Knowledge: Control

In the preceding section, we described the structure of knowledge representation, but in order to understand action taken, it is also necessary to describe how different types of knowledge are related to a subject's control of the mental activity on which action is based. *Automatic information processing* is a learnt response which is triggered by certain signs in the surrounding world. It is fast and difficult to suppress or change when it has first been learnt (McLaughlin 1987:134).

If we compare this with the revised ACT* model, it corresponds to the description of the processing found in production memory. The advantage is fast processing, which is not attentionally controlled by the subject and therefore demands very little mental energy (see above). The price paid for this efficiency is the lack of flexibility in use.

The opposite situation occurs in relation to *controlled processing*, which is consciously controlled by the subject. It is - as opposed to parallel, automatic processing - serial. It demands much capacity but has the advantage of being easy to establish and adapt to new situations (McLaughlin 1987:135).

Automised information processing is characterised by learnt knowledge not being open to changes via a change of the rules of the programme, as there are no explicit rules. If behaviour is to be changed a new training phase is necessary in order to internalise new knowledge. On the other hand, already incorporated data may be generalised to new data within the same area of knowledge (see for example Rumelhart, McClelland *et al*, 1986 and McClelland, Rumelhart *et al*, 1986). This means that in a way this type of knowledge is rule-based as well. *Rule-based* knowledge - whether based on restructuring (compiling) or on generalisation of automised knowledge - becomes the creative knowledge *per se* where knowledge-based and skill-based knowledge meet.

Our model of knowledge representation can be summarised as follows:

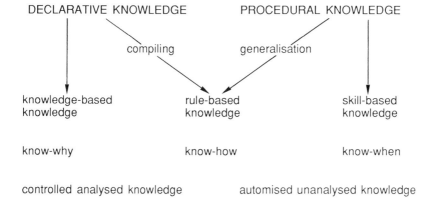

DECLARATIVE KNOWLEDGE   PROCEDURAL KNOWLEDGE

compiling   generalisation

knowledge-based   rule-based   skill-based
knowledge   knowledge   knowledge

know-why   know-how   know-when

controlled analysed knowledge   automised unanalysed knowledge

Figure 2

All three types of knowledge and both types of processing are important in relation to translation tasks. Automised knowledge caters for the lower levels of production, i.e. the elements of the task, where the informant has stored patterns of behaviour, which on the basis of unanalysed knowledge are triggered by certain signs in the task. Rule-based knowledge sees to the more routine-like conscious processing, i.e. the combination of automised sub-routines. Finally knowledge-based, declarative knowledge takes care of problem solving which is based on metalinguistic knowledge in analysed symbols systems.

The categories of analysis are all included in the figure below, which shows the development of translation competence: the most effective use of analysed and automised knowledge.

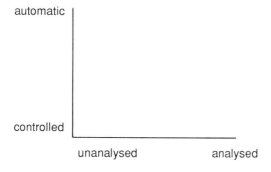

automatic

controlled

unanalysed   analysed

Figure 3

The combination between serial and parallel processing is not only the most likely one, it is also the most efficient and flexible one. In relation to task solution this is reflected in the subject's ability to change focus from *form* to *content*. The more automised low level task solution is, the more time is left for overall planning and high level problem solving.

6.0 Data

As we stated in our section on design, we have three types of data: loud-thinking, retrospection and written text. Examples of loud-thinking and retrospection data are included in the following section together with analyses of data; the introspection was done in Danish - the Ll of the informants - the examples included below have been translated into English. The protocols are very long, and it is not possible to reproduce them here or to analyse them on all points of potential interest. The analysis in the following sections will focus on the solutions offered to one grammatical problem: future reference by means of present tense or future tense *going to* / *will* + progressive, and two lexical problems. The following conventions are used:

____	underlining	indicates English words that are used in the translation or suggested as possible solutions
'...'	single quotation marks	indicates Danish text
-	dash	indicates a pause
...	dots	indicates an unfinished utterance
(...)	bracketed dots	indicates excluded text

I = the informant

R = the researcher

To ease the identification of the following extracts, the following notation is used: informants are indicated by group adherence and letter of identification, H refers to loud-thinking protocol extracts, R refers to retrospection data. For instance: lAH = Group 1, Informant A, loud-thinking protocol extract.

Below we find the first and last clauses of the text that the informants were asked to translate from Danish into English. After that the individual informant's translation is included, in the form in which it was handed in.

The following apply to these translations:

* = changed into the following word
** = deleted.

6.1 Danish Text

Den britisk-franske Concorde flyver i de kommende uger ind i en uvis fremtid, nøje overvåget af den britiske regering, som til efteråret træffer afgørelse om Concorde-projektets skæbne.
Så vil briterne konstatere, hvad et supersonisk brag vil sige, når maskinen flyver ned gennem en korridor mellem Irland og England.

6.2 Translations

Group 1 Informant A

In the coming weeks, the British-French Concorde will fly into an unknown future - closely followed by the British government, who are to decide about the future* fate of the Concorde project this autumn.
Then the English will observe what a** supersonic noise is like, when the aircraft flies through a corridor between Ireland and England.

Group 1 Informant L

During the next few weeks the Gr** British-French Concorde will fly into an uncertain future closely* under close surveillance by the British government, who will decide on the fate of the Concorde-project in the autumn.
Then the British will experience the sound of** a supersonic boom when the plane will fly* flies down a corridor between Ireland and England.

Group 2 Informant D

The British-French Concorde will fly into an uncertain future in the weeks to come. It will be carefully surveyed by the British government which will make a decision about the fate of the Concorde project in the autumn.
When the aircraft flies down a corridor between Ireland and Great Britain the British will find out what a supersonic bang means.

Group 2 Informant G

The British-French Concorde flyes into an uncertain future in the upcoming weeks - closely surveyed by the British government. The government makes the decision of the faith of the Concorde-project this autumn.

When the plane passes through a corridor between Ireland and England, the British population is going to learn what a supersonic bang is.

7.0 Analysis

The following analysis is based on the division into knowledge types which was outlined above under Production. The three types of knowledge are:

- knowledge-based knowledge
- rule-based knowledge
- skill-based knowledge.

In the analysis, the four informants' information processing is discussed relative to the three knowledge types. We also comment on:

- the analysis and control dimensions
- the informants' task focus
- the informants' inter-language.

7.1 Analysis and Control

The four informants all use all three types of knowledge and both dimensions in task solution, i.e. the dimensions of analysis and control, see Figure 3 and cf. Schneider and Schiffrin quoted above. Below we outline an information processing profile for each informant.

The Group 1 informants command a good deal of analysed knowledge. This is particularly clear from their retrospections where they expand on their reasons for selecting a particular option, but 1A verbalises analysed knowledge as early as the loud-thinking stage. 1A's use of analysed knowledge is prominent in her approach to syntactic problems (here: future reference and word order), where she verbalises knowledge-based knowledge in relation to a problem-space which she establishes:

Example 1 (1AH)
And 'flyver' that is neutral future reference, we must remember that, future tense: will fly.

The informant uses less analysed knowledge in relation to lexical problems, where she operates more on the basis of skill-based knowledge:

Example 2 (1AH)
And then we have got the 'brag' left. We have said crash, we have said bang and we have rejected large and big noise. Right now I cannot think of anything because I cannot remember anything in relation to the word 'brag'.

IL also operates on the basis of analysed knowledge, but however, she does not use knowledge-based knowledge, but rule-based knowledge; it does not have the same depth as 1A's knowledge. The retrospection shows, however, that the informant commands compiled, knowledge-based knowledge. Simultaneously with this compiling, a skill-based knowledge representation has been established so that the informant no longer has access to / commands detailed, metalinguistically formulated knowledge.

Example 3 (1LH)
The British-French Concorde 'flyver' will fly into an unknown future.

Example 4 (1LR)
R: Then you have the expression 'flyver i de kommende uger', there you said very quickly: future: will.
I: Yes, reference is made to the coming weeks, it has not happened yet, then Danish often has present tense for future reference which English does not have as often.
R: Did you consider this particularly much? Besides the argumentation that you came up with while writing down, or was it more - ?
I: No, it came more or less by itself, because you have had it dinned into your head so often.

The informant's analysed knowledge is characterised by rules-of-thumb, and in Example 4 they provide sufficient information for the informant to solve the task. This is not the case in the following example. She reaches a correct solution, but based on rule-based knowledge and she therefore cannot explain why.

Example 5 (1LR)
R: (The last sentence): 'når maskinen flyver ned gennem en korridor mellem England og Irland' there you said: it is some sort of of future tense.
I: Yes, I really considered the same as I did in the first sentence, that it does so somewhere in the near future, but the interesting point is that I do not stick to it, and fairly soon I discovered that I had forgotten it above, I inserted it and removed the other one.

R: Why?

I: I really do not know, they were too close so ... I believe that I tend to ... I like compact language, and why should I then point out twice within one type-written line that this is future tense. I believe it is part of the explanation. But I cannot explain why I kept it in the first sentence.

R: Could it be related to the structure of the sentence? Or, what type of sentence is it?

I: The subjunctive? No, I believe that it is a subordinate time clause. Well, I do not know. It relates to my concentrating on the words and then theoretical grammar is not my strong point, sometimes I am able to identify a mistake, but I cannot really explain.

It is characteristic of both groups of informants that they have a wide range of considerations in relation to their vocabulary; these considerations are often linked to a wish for lexical and stylistic variation and the precise rendering of single words / phrases.

Example 6 (1AH)
I prefer in the weeks to come, but it is a bit old-fashioned and stiff. We'll write as it says: In the coming weeks.

Example 7 (1LH)
And then I have to find out what 'brag' is, and it has something to do with quality, it is not quality, but that type of word. And 'supersonisk' must be the same, I guess, and before I said boom; it is pure guesswork and one may rely too much on that, because when I say boom I cannot think of anything but economy and a supersonic bang sounds childish; what else could 'brag' be, this is nasty, I think.

A comparison of the two Group 1 informants' characteristic information processing shows that the major difference between the two is that of automatisation. 1A has automised a smaller part of her analysed knowledge than 1L: she operates in a more controlled way and she defines her problem-spaces explicitly.

Example 8 (1AH)
And 'flyver', I wonder whether this is also future reference. No, you cannot say when the aircraft will fly. No, there is some rule about a relative clause, then we do not need compound tenses, or something like that. I really ought to be able to remember this.

1L draws a higher number of informed conclusions, and via compiling - she has automised more of the knowledge-based input that she has been exposed to during her education. She therefore operates on a less controlled basis.

As expected, the Group 2 informants use less analysed knowledge than Group 1. This is primarily linked to their educational background (see section on Informants). Their loud-thinking has little verbalisation but the retrospection has more. It is characteristic that the Group 2 informants use skill-based and rule-based knowledge, which they try to use for explanation purposes in the retrospection.

Example 9 (2DR)
I had a good deal of discussion with myself about <u>will</u> and <u>going to</u> etc, and about which is better here. In the event it was at random after all, I think.

Example 10 (2GR)
R: You wrote: <u>the government makes the decision of the faith of the Concorde-project this summer</u>. Now that we are discussing tense, what tense of the verb have you got here? In the Danish text it says: 'som til efteråret træffer afgørelse'.
I: In principle the two are alike, I think, it is also...
R: And what do you mean by that?
I: Well, it should have said: <u>the government is going to make a decision of the faith of the Concorde-project this autumn</u>.
R: Can you explain why?
I: Why? It is because I realise ... or autumn is ... you might as well, if it is winter now - if you imagine that it was winter now, and you were writing now, then you could still say: this autumn. No, then it would have said - No, no it does not work. But in this situation. I do not think that it can be misunderstood, this looks ... No, it is no good either. What I would have said is that is was, it is <u>this autumn</u>, it could also be used about the autumn that was, or has been, although (...) that is the same, that is, for instance <u>this spring</u>, isn't it; it could be something that had happened. But you cannot use it here.

There is a significant difference between the two informants, however. 2D operates on the basis of rule-based knowledge. He commands some syntactic rules-of-thumb, among other things as regards word-order and the expression of future meaning in English, and he is able to define a problem-space by means of this rule-based knowledge.

Example 11 (2DH)
I think I have a small problem here, there is future reference in 'når maskinen flyver', but on the other hand, <u>when the machine will fly</u>, that is too heavy - I think I'll use ordinary present tense instead.

With regard to lexical problems, 2D primarily operates on the basis of skill-based knowledge; this can be seen from the following example:

Example 12 (2DH)
'Hvad et supersonisk brag vil sige': <u>what a supersonic boom</u> - that sounds silly, <u>crash</u>, no that has a different character. There is probably a fixed expression for 'et supersonisk brag'. I would probably try to look it up, but so far I'll choose <u>boom</u>, <u>Bang</u>, well, <u>bang</u> sounds better.

2G operates on the basis of unanalysed knowledge. He does not define local problem-spaces, and the global problem is just translation as such - not a particular type of translation which entails a specific response.

Example 13 (2GH)
And then I'll try to write down what I have found out about; if it does not work then we'll have to correct it: <u>decision</u>. And then there is one of these words, well, I suppose I have to. OK, I'll write it: <u>decision</u>.

The informant uses quick, skill-based decisions concerning a particular translation item. He is primarily interested in conveying the meaning of words, phrases and entire sentences, rather than in detailed translation. He uses automised, skill-based knowledge for this, and it is often not sufficient to solve the task in question.

Example 14 (2GH)
Well. 'Den britisk-franske Concorde flyver i de kommende uger ind i en uvis fremtid, nøje overvåget af den britiske regering.' The beginning is not too problematic, it is quite straightforward. 'Flyver' ... <u>fly</u>, I believe. So then: <u>flys</u>.

If we place our informants in the model outlined in Figure 3 we get the following figure:

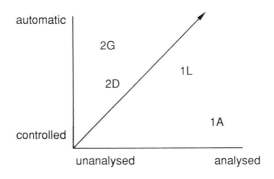

Figure 4

The figure shows how our informants use the two dimensions differently. 1A and 2D both operate in a more controlled manner than the other two informants. They both produce a controlled response, but on the basis of analysed knowledge that is used differently (see Examples 1 and 11). 2D primarily controls via rule-based knowledge, 1A uses knowledge-based knowledge, that is, knowledge that is more analysed in character. The other two informants, 1L and 2G, use the control dimension considerably less, both as regards syntax and vocabulary. This is particularly the case with 2G who almost entirely uses skill-based knowledge, whereas 1L - like 2D - uses rule-based knowledge as well. The extent and type of analysed knowledge commanded by the informants differ, but the two informants resemble each other as regards their fairly extensive use of automised knowledge.

Example 15 (1LH)
... then the British will experience the supersonic ... when the plane flies down the corridor between Ireland and England; for some reason or other I resent changing my initial - somewhat risky - solution that the word is boom (...) I think that I'll stick to boom, it is a general word, and maybe it relates to the fact that I use much 'economic language'; I wonder if it is complete nonsense, but then it is just too bad.

7.2 Informants' Task Focus

Our second point of analysis relates to the informants' attitude to the task, their evaluation of the problem-space(s) in question, and their work with these problem-spaces. The Group 1 informants are very much alike in this respect: they concentrate on form. They focus on individual items in their linguistic and contextual rendering of the source text, and the major part of their problem-solving activities is focused on producing a translation which is as close to the source text as possible. Examples 1 and 7 show this focus on form and on correctness both as regards syntax and vocabulary. 1A often defines problem-spaces by using knowledge-based knowledge, she uses grammatical terminology in task solution (the text as symbol, see Example 8). 1L operates in a less controlled and less analysed way and therefore uses more rule- and skill-based knowledge (the text as signs, Example 5).

The Group 2 informants work from meaning to form. They concentrate on the context and produce - on the basis of what is syntactically and lexically within their reach - a contextually based version of the source text. They simultaneously change the form of the text in order to solve the task.

Example 16 (2GH)
Then I think that I'll put a full stop here and then start out by changing a relative clause into a main clause. Then I'll move the constituents around a bit in order to make it work. (See also Example 1).

The Group 2 informants do not use knowledge-based rules for problem solving itself, but in particular 2D uses rule-based knowledge to explain and support a given task solution (Example 11), while 2G uses content and context to explain his skill-based solutions (Example 10). It is characteristic that 2D uses rules-of-thumb to produce and explain, whereas 2G uses content / context to explain - not produce - the response in question.

Our four informants' problem-solving strategies are different. In the loud-thinking 1A operates on the basis of knowledge, and the text is interpreted as symbols that constitute a theoretical framework for the search process. The solution selected can therefore be argued for in metalinguistic terms. 1L and 2D use rule-based knowledge. The text is interpreted as signs and a less well-defined problem-space and less clear-cut solutions follow from this approach. 2G uses skill-based knowledge almost entirely, as this knowledge is limited, the sign interpretation of the text leads to one solution only.

7.3 Informants' Interlanguage

The informants' interlanguage will be commented on from two points of view: first, its distance from the L2 norm and secondly, the use of L1, L2 and transfer in task solutions.

The Group 1 informants' solutions come close to the target language norm, with regard to both syntax and vocabulary (see written translations in section on Data). They produce adequate translations of the source text. The Group 2 informants are further away from the target language norm; 2D primarily with regard to vocabulary, where he uses less stylistic variation than the Group 1 informants. 2G deviates with regard to both syntax and vocabulary. 2G's automised use of primarily unanalysed knowledge is not sufficient to solve the task adequately.

Example 17 (2GH)
Well, 'flyver' it can be used both in the physical sense of flies, and in a more figurative meaning, but it is probably the more physical fly - fly I guess. That is: flys. No, it probably has an -es. Normally I would look that up, check which is correct. But I am certain that it has an -es.

It is characteristic that syntax is the major troublemaker to this informant. When rule-based knowledge is included, he operates on the basis of observed regularities; he establishes some content-based guidelines that are then generalised to cover the entire problem-solving task. In the retrospection he concludes that the text refers to the future. He observes that he used is going to to express future meaning and he then generalises on this basis. His conclusion is that he ought to have used 'these ing-forms' for all future reference examples in the text.

Example 18 (2GR)

R: Flies?
I: Yes, I think if it has an i, then it is the insect.
R: This word has an i as well. Talking about the verb, did you consider anything in particular in relation to this sentence: The British Concorde flies into an uncertain future?
I: Well, yes I should have, I can see that now, because I did that later.
R: Yes you did - you considered it later.
I: Because I have used the 'ing-forms' there, I ought to have done that here as well: is flying into.
R: I see; can you explain why you would select that?
I: Because the ing-form, I believe it is used when when something is happening, something happening now and which goes on in the future. And then I ought to have used it here as well.
R: That is, you would like to use is flying to indicate what?
I: To indicate that this is something that happens from now on and then onwards.
R: Something that is going to happen, I see.
I: That is future reference.

As we can see from Examples 17 and 18, 2G operates on the basis of a strategy in his loud-thinking which is: transfer from Danish if possible. Transfer is his initial suggestion as regards future reference (see also Example 14). When he includes rule-based knowledge in the retrospection, provoked by the researcher's question, he tries to describe his rule on the basis of content, not form (Example 10).

With regard to vocabulary, he has several L2-based strategies of solution. This relates well to his extensive use of contextual, skill-based knowledge and his translation ends up being markedly different from the other informants' translations with regard to syntactic and lexical correctness (see his written translation in the Data section).

This takes us to the use of L1 and L2 and transfer by the other informants. lL and 2D use the L2 the most - in the control phase their evaluation is closely related to whether something 'sounds correct', but 2D also has examples of transfer. 2D distinguishes himself from 2G in so far as the examples of transfer are instances of positive transfer. IL and 2D base the majority of their rules on L2 rules (see Example 9) and they only operate on a contrastive basis in a few cases.

Example 19 (ILR)

R: You also make use of the expression: it sounds correct. What makes you say so?

I: It is intuition only, it has no relation to what I may have learnt. I don't know if it is related to books that I have read, where some phrases are remembered. I love reading aloud to myself at home. I adore the charming expressions used.

R: You say yourself that your intuition takes precedence in the cases where you feel that something sounds better or something looks wrong; do you ever use more formal rules to check whether your intuition is correct?

I: Hardly ever.

Example 20 (2DH)

Well, I have to look at this; find out if I can use the same syntax as in Danish. I think that at any rate I have to put 'i de kommende uger' at the end of the first sentence. Yes, that is necessary - but otherwise it is almost as it is in Danish.

1A is different. She relates her solutions to her L1 by means of grammatical rules which resemble the rules found in grammar textbooks. She works on the basis of Danish grammar textbooks about English and she often uses a contrastive approach. She uses controlled, knowledge-based rules, as we find in the following example:

Example 21 (1AH)

Closely followed by the British government. And then I believe that an ordinary relative clause can be used here, and government; we have to look at it as plural here, and then I said - I cannot remember what I said. I am saying that I will write who are to decide. That is a good English construction, it doesn't relate to hitting with a gun [*træffe* can be used in both contexts in Danish - our comment]. Change their decision, we change the wordclass, that was my statement before. Who are to decide ... I'll write that ... we write who are to decide about the future, it was not future but fate even though it is in the future: who are to decide about the ... fate of the Concorde project.

The informants' interlanguage and task focus are clearly influenced by their educational backgrounds and their personal style: whether they focus more on content than form or vice versa, whether they trust their feeling for the correct solution, whether they work in a controlled way and whether they define and perceive the task set in a particular way. These factors are furthermore influenced by the informants' knowledge representation and a very complex picture is the result.

7.4 Summary of Analyses

Our analyses show that there are characteristic differences between the four informants' task solutions. 2G solves the task in the shortest time. This is caused by his extensive use of unanalysed and automised skill-based knowledge. He has a problem, however; he has too little analysed and controlled rule-based or knowledge-based knowledge. This is particularly a problem as his skill-based knowledge is insufficient and automatisation has been based on transfer of L1 knowledge.

The contrast to this informant is 1A, who has the longest task solution. This is caused by her extensive use of analysed and controlled knowledge-based L2 knowledge. Both 1L and 2D are characterised by using a good deal of automised, skill-based knowledge which is coupled with some analysed and controlled knowledge of the rule-based type in their task solutions. They distinguish themselves from each other with regard to the character of their rule-based knowledge. 1L seems to be an example of the learner who has compiled knowledge-based knowledge (see section on Informants (Group 1) and Example 4). This makes her focus on form (the 'charming expressions', see Example 19). 2D is more liable to generalise from observed regularities; this can be seen in his use of transfer (cf. 2G). 2D's use of this approach leads to positive transfer, however.

Our model, see Figure 2, which outlined the ideal development of a translator's competence, showed that the competent translator uses both automised and analysed L2 knowledge. This means that to the extent possible, the translator uses automised knowledge representations. They are used in an unanalysed form in a task solution when this solution proceeds without any problems. But the competent translator is also able to leave the automatic processing and change to more attention-demanding rule-based and knowledge-based knowledge representation when this is deemed necessary. The shift takes place as the result of an identification and delineation of problem-spaces.

Our overview of the informants' position relative to the ideal translator's competence shows (see Figure 4) that none of our four informants comply with ideal demands. 1A works in a very controlled way and based on analysed knowledge, but she lacks belief in her own skill-based knowledge, and she therefore ends up making the task more difficult for herself than necessary; she actually solves the task twice. She is - to use Krashen's terminology - a Monitor overuser (Krashen 1985). 2G is the absolute contrast to 1A. He hardly uses anything but skill-based knowledge, and this knowledge is often both insufficient and contradictory to the L2 norm. The retrospection shows, however, that he does command a good deal of rule-based knowledge (Example 18). If this knowledge had been used in the loud-thinking it might have prevented certain unsuccessful solutions. In Krashen's terminology he is a Monitor underuser (Krashen 1985). Both 1L and 2D base their solutions on skill-based and rule-based knowledge. They differ from each other as regards task focus: 1L focuses on form, e.g. in the form of stylistic considerations introduced in order to produce a correct translation; 2D focuses more on content and is satisfied with a translation which conveys the meaning of the source text. They both lack the ability to include knowledge-based knowledge; this type of knowledge might have provided the informants with the knowledge necessary for producing the optimum translation. It is a joint characteristic for all four informants that the initial response to the task set is based on skill-based and rule-based knowledge.

Example 22 (1AH)
Now, I am going to try to read aloud a rough draft of the translation into English that I have in mind.

Knowledge-based knowledge - as we find in 1A's protocol - is used as a checking device in relation to an initial draft. Skill-based and rule-based knowledge thus become the central types of knowledge representation. Knowledge-based knowledge is introduced to the extent that the informant has access to it and considers it necessary for production. This is shown by our Figure 4 of the informants' position relative to our ideal translator's profile. 1L and 2D are characterised by shifts between skill-based and rule-based knowledge; they are then both 'effective' translators compared to the time they invest in producing the translation, their linguistic competence and the result reached, and they therefore come closest to the ideal translator's development that we have outlined.

8 Pedagogic Perspectives

Our conclusions about the four informants' information processing above show *inter alia* that the best results are reached when the learners have access to analysed knowledge in the situations where they experience difficulties in relation to task solution. This means that they can retrieve rules that tell them why a grammatical problem should be solved in a particular way. Their grammatical knowledge is characterised by resembling grammar textbook rules, and it has probably been acquired in the classroom. Another result is that the use of unanalysed skill-based knowledge is prominent when task solution poses no problems.

This means that L2 instruction, which is aimed at assisting advanced learners, should take into account both the acquisition of sufficient analysed knowledge and sufficient skill-based knowledge. If we look at this from a pedagogical point of view, it means that grammar instruction is necessary as it supports the learner's task solution and his / her understanding of why. It enables the learner to establish his / her own interlanguage rules, which in our data are often rules-of-thumb that can be applied easily in task solution, i.e. the rules are of the know-how type (see Figure 2). Grammar instruction appears to assist the learner in his / her identification of problem-spaces and selection of relevant approach to the task, especially at the know-how level.

One of the aims of L2 grammar instruction is to contribute to making grammatical knowledge conscious and to turn it into a useful tool in task solution. This can be done in different ways, depending on which view of the psychological processes involved in learning the teacher or researcher holds. It is our opinion that with reference to attaining translation competence, learning the grammar of the L2 should be seen as an aid to language learning, not an object of learning; grammatical knowledge should assist in, but not control, task solution (compare Informants 1L and 1A; 1L uses her grammatical knowledge to assist her in task solution, but without letting this type of knowledge dominate). *Grammar should assist in the establishment of problem-solving strategies, but it should not be the strategy itself.*

How can grammar instruction be adapted to learner-centred demands? How can the pedagogic grammar, which is selective by definition, be used in the most fruitful way by the teachers of foreign languages and advanced learners who wish to become able translators? The following could be suggested. The grammar textbooks used should enable the learners to focus on chunks of language which are larger than the word, i.e. phrases, clauses and entire paragraphs; a discourse-oriented type of grammar is assumed to assist the learner in a better way than the well-known word- and sentence-based grammar. Individual components of the language are assumed to be part of the advanced learner's knowledge already, so grammar at this level of description is only relevant or necessary in very few cases.

The ideal grammar textbook for the advanced learner is therefore - in our opinion - oriented towards the process, aimed at increasing the learner's understanding of the language as a whole, and focused on the acquisition of knowledge of the know-why and know-how type. In our opinion the starting-point in grammar instruction for advanced learners should be the kind of grammatical knowledge the learner may benefit from in a task solution. The learner should be able to use this knowledge and to apply it when necessary, e.g. when skill-based / know-when knowledge does not suffice. The central point becomes the ability to recognise the usefulness of introducing grammatical knowledge in situations where this is necessary to ensure *correctness* in task solution. As far as we know there is no single and unified answer, no existing grammar textbook that will provide the information that we are looking for: the problem-solving assistance which enters into the production of the output (here: the translation). However, the following elements of grammar instruction related to translation could be considered:

- focus on the contribution that grammatical knowledge can make to problematic task solutions;
- the introduction of contrastively-based rules in task solution to avoid negative transfer;
- the possibility of getting confirmation of already established hypotheses, e.g. useful rules-of-thumb.

These elements of grammar instruction / a grammar textbook may contribute to motivating learners for using grammatical knowledge as a source of information when this is necessary and they may contribute to learners trusting their own skill-based knowledge in cases where no problems occur during task solution.

9 Conclusions

The ability to use skill-based knowledge does not develop by itself, however. The advanced learner should be exposed to translation tasks that enhance automatisation, e.g. tasks whose complexity is mainly at the phrase, sentence and paragraph levels rather than at the the level of the word. To reach this level of high automatisation, other activities / tasks are relevant as well; no doubt useful assistance can be gained from the introduction of, for example, spontaneous oral presentations that demand the use of skill-based knowledge in production.

As outlined, we believe that in the learning process, the introduction of rule-based knowledge (know-how knowledge) is central and here the discourse grammar suggested above is a good tool. As regards the use of acquired knowledge in production, the optimal Monitor-user (Krashen 1985) relies mainly on skill-based knowledge but is able to introduce rule-based and knowledge-based knowledge in cases where she / he experiences difficulties. The main task for the teacher is therefore to enhance the learner's awareness of the potential but also of the limitations of their current linguistic competence.

Notes

1. In this article the term introspection is used as a general term to denote both informants' loud-thinking and retrospection.

Bibliography

Anderson, J.R. (1983) *The Architecture of Cognition.* Cambridge, Mass.: Harvard University Press.

Anderson, J.R. (1985) *Cognitive Psychology and its Implications.* New York: Freeman.

Bialystok, E. (1982) On the Relationship between Knowing and Using Linguistic Forms. *Applied Linguistics*: 3,3: pp.181-207.

Brunak, S. and Lautrup, B. (1988) *Neurale Netværk.* København: Munksgaard.

Börsch, S. (1986) Introspective Methods in research on Interlingual and Intercultural Communication in Blum-Kulka, S. and House, J. (eds.) *Interlingual and Intercultural Communication.* Tübingen: Narr.

Chomsky, N. (1988) *Language and the Problems of Knowledge.* Cambridge, Mass: MIT Press.

Ericsson, K.A. and Simon, H.A. (1984) *Protocol Analysis: Verbal Reports on Data.* Cambridge, Mass: MIT Press.

Gardner, H. (1987) *The Mind's New Science.* New York: Basic Books Inc.

Jacobs, B. (1988) Neurobiological Differentiation of Primary and Secondary Language Acquisition. *SSLA* 10,3: pp.281-303.

Jensen, K. A. and Kiel, E. (1988) Innateness and Language Acquisition. *Pluridicta* 10.

Johnson-Laird, P.N. (1983) *Mental Models: Towards a Cognitive Science of Language, Inference and Consciousness.* Cambridge: Cambridge University Press.

Johnson-Laird, P.N. (1988) *The Computer and the Mind.* London: Fontana.

Krashen, S. D. (1985) *The Input Hypothesis: Issues and Implications.* London: Longman.

McClelland, J.L., Rumelhart, D.E. et al. (1986) *Parallel Distributed Processing. Exploration in the Microstructures of Cognition*, Vol 2: Psychological and Biological Models. Cambridge, Mass: MIT Press.

McLaughlin, B. (1987) *Theories of Second-Language Learning.* London: E. Arnold.

Nisbett, R.E. and Wilson, T.L. (1977) Telling More than We Can Know: Verbal Reports on Mental Processes. *Psychological Review*, 84: pp.231-259.

Rasmussen, J. (1987) *Mental Models and the Control of Actions in Complex Environments.* Risø.

Rumelhart, D.E., McClelland J.L. et al. (1986) *Parallel Distributed Processing. Explorations in the Microstructures of Cognition*, Vol 1: Foundations. Cambridge. Mass: MIT Press.

Schiffrin, R.M. and Schneider, R.W. (1984) Automatic and Controlled Processing Revisited. *Psychological Review* 91, 2: pp.269-276.

Stillings, N.A. et al. (1989) *Cognitive Science. An Introduction.* Cambridge, Mass: MIT Press.

Testing the Test:
a preliminary investigation of translation as a test of writing skills

Shirley Larsen

1. Introduction

The history of translation is long and distinguished and no one would deny the value and importance of this particular skill, especially in the modern world, where so much of our written material is translated. A great deal of this work is done by professional translators, who, as far as possible, translate into the mother tongue. Klein-Brayley and Smith (1985:160), writing about the situation in Western Germany, say: 'Professional translators either work into their own language or have their work checked by a native speaker of L2 if they translate in the other direction'.[1] Nevertheless, much translating into a foreign language is also done by people who are not professional, in the sense that their work does not primarily consist in translating. Some of this is good, some adequate and some lamentable, as we all know from, for instance, business correspondence, tourist brochures and labels on tins. (For a long time I treasured a small tin of curry powder which instructed me to 'Take chicken. Cut him in four ...') There is, then, a lot to be said for translation, in both directions, forming part of a University degree course in a foreign language. This is a skill that the graduate may well be called upon to employ in his future career, and one, moreover, that he will automatically be assumed to possess.

The latter point is not without importance. To many people, proficiency in a foreign language and the ability to translate go hand in hand, presumably because for many years translation occupied a central position in the teaching of foreign languages. Writing skills were both taught and tested through the medium of translation. This is no longer the case, but translation still forms part of the language teaching apparatus at various levels, despite the scorn that has been poured on it over the past few decades. It has been both supported and condemned for identical reasons. Some people defend it as a means of testing the learner's control of specific linguistic features; others castigate this particular application of translation. Many people find it helpful in the teaching of language proficiency, this being the group that favours a contrastive approach (as I do), whereas others maintain that it impedes the acquisition of the foreign language. In two other articles in this volume, Knud Sørensen and Flemming Olsen make out a strong case for the pedagogical value of translation exercises. It is, however, as a test of general language proficiency that translation has been most criticized. In their article on translation as a testing procedure, Klein-Braley and Smith quote a number of researchers, including Lado (1961:32), who claims that:

> The ability to translate is a special skill. People who speak a foreign language well are not necessarily those that translate most effectively, although there is a correlation between knowledge of the foreign language and the capacity to translate.[2]

They also quote Collier and Shields (1977:7):

> There is often a discrepancy between mediocre performance in translation classes on the one hand, and highly proficient work in oral and composition classes on the other.[3]

This I would endorse from my own experience, although I would go further and claim that the reverse can, to some extent at least, also be true.

However, this is only a personal impression and as such completely uninteresting. I decided, then, that I would take a closer look at the performance of University students in translation exercises and in free production. It so happens that I have a number of copies of examination scripts from the Part I (*bifag/1. del*) examination in Written English at the University of Aarhus, and it is on these that I have based my investigation - which is not yet complete: indeed, so far I have merely scratched the surface.

2. The Investigation

Until 1986, the examination in Written English, a six-hour paper, consisted of a summary, a translation and an essay. The candidate was given two 1,200-word articles in Danish (usually from a newspaper) to choose between, and was required to summarize the whole text in English in approximately 250 words, translate a given passage of about 250 words and write an essay on a topic of his own choosing, provided it was connected with the article; a particular essay topic was, however, suggested. The purpose of the examination was, of course, to test the candidate's ability to write fluent, correct and idiomatic English. The summary was to be written in a sober, neutral style, the translation was to reproduce the style of the source language text, whereas in the essay the candidate was free to choose his own style, although this was expected to be appropriate to the subject and the way in which he tackled it. It was felt that this particular type of examination constituted a good all-round test of the candidate's language proficiency, moving from controlled production in the translation to semi-controlled in the summary and to completely free production in the essay.

No examination is perfect and this particular one was no exception. To begin with, it is not easy to find 1,200-word articles, which meant that in most cases we had to doctor the texts, cutting out chunks and rewriting the odd sentence in the interests of cohesion and coherence. (Admittedly, when the examination was introduced in 1974, the articles were 2,000 words in length, corresponding to the average *kronik* in a Danish newspaper, but it proved difficult to cope with the summary (350 words) of such a long text in the time available).

Secondly, no dictionaries or aids of any kind were allowed, with the result that a number of potentially interesting and suitable texts had to be discarded, as they contained too much specialized vocabulary. We could, of course, gloss the occasional word, as indeed we did, but not more than two or three.

Thirdly, a well-written, carefully-structured text is not necessarily easy to summarize under examination conditions, as it may well contain too little redundancy. A number of the examination texts were, then, loosely structured and sometimes sloppily written, which did not matter as regards the summary and the essay, but did pose problems when it came to selecting a suitable passage for translation. Some of the translation passages were therefore difficult to render into good English, simply because the Danish was not always as good as it might have been. There are two schools of thought here, the one being that examinees should not be expected to translate poorly written texts, the other being that in a real life situation one is frequently required to translate texts that deviate from the linguistic norms, and an examinee should be able to demonstrate his ability to cope with such texts. I have always adhered to the latter school, but now, having reread a number of examination scripts, I feel that in some instances we were perhaps expecting the students to bite off rather more than they could chew.

Finally, and this is probably the most serious objection to the examination, the candidates were not required to write for a particular audience or for a particular purpose. The inevitable sense of writing in a vacuum is likely to have had an effect on the candidates' performance in all three parts of the paper, and especially in the essay, which they almost invariably dealt with last. At this stage, towards the end of what was a demanding, indeed a gruelling examination, a number of them had difficulty in conjuring up interesting ideas or genuine opinions and this was bound to affect their written English.

I have gone into what I consider the shortcomings of this examination at what may seem tedious length, because I think they may have a bearing on my investigation. In other words, I am questioning the extent to which the examination provided *ideal* conditions for testing the candidates' written English, and this must in its turn have an effect on the investigation itself. It is not that I think that this particular form of examination is a bad one; on the contrary, there is much to recommend it, simply because it looks at different *types* of language production. What I do question is a) writing for nobody in particular, b) the significance of the translation passage.

The investigation is on the face of it simple and straight-forward: it entails comparing the English produced by the candidates in the translation with that produced in the summary and the essay. In actual fact, the task is by no means simple and straightforward, as the passages set for translation varied considerably and did not always enable the candidate to demonstrate his command of the language to the full. There could, for instance, be a great difference between the type of structures and lexical items called for in the translation and those that the candidate was able to use in free production. I have, then, primarily concentrated on certain linguistic areas where Danes tend to have problems, together with a few other features which seemed to me to be significant. Inevitably, there are a number of areas which remain unexplored, such as the type of sentence structure demanded in the translation compared with what the candidate was able to produce himself - and here I am thinking of both complexity and variety. Neither have I as yet gone into vocabulary in any detail, or into such aspects as the appropriate choice of words, the idiomatic use of language, or, indeed, whether the language used sounds natural. All of these are important features of written English, which I hope to look into at a later stage.

Finally, I should like to emphasize that I am dealing with a very small sample. The bulk of the investigation concentrates on the work of 34 candidates in connection with five different articles. I have used only examination scripts that I have assessed myself, simply because this made my work easier, as I could understand my own method of marking mistakes and what I considered good formulations.

I shall start by giving an example of the kind of English that is sometimes produced in an essay. The candidate is discussing pollution and what can be done to combat it:

> What we usually do about the deliberate outled of toxicated water are to sue the companies. But since our legislation, apart from being very slow on these matters (as so many tests has to be undertaken), is lenient as to the amount of the fine presented to the company after the trial, the company can almost in any case, gain a profit by leading out toxicated water which is at least ten times higher than the fine.

It should, admittedly, be borne in mind that the candidate had no dictionary and so could not look up such words as *toksisk* and *udledning*. It would also seem, however, that he did not know the exact meaning of 'legislation', yet he was able to use this word correctly in the translation:

> The cooperation between neighbouring countries meant that the local consumers' movements were able to put pressure on the authorities for better legislation ...

> (Samarbejdet mellem nabolandene betød, at de lokale bevægelser kunne presse myndighederne til at gennemtvinge langt bedre love ...)

In fact, the translation was reasonable, with comparatively few mistakes of vocabulary and structure, and no elementary mistakes apart from one of punctuation and one of spelling. Thus there were no mistakes of concord, whereas there were six in the 400-word essay (including: 'you pollutes'), together with other mistakes of the type that occur in the extract quoted above. This was one of the examination scripts that made me begin to wonder if translation was an adequate test of the ability to write acceptable English.[4]

One swallow, as they say, does not make a summer, and one student's examination script is not enough to base any judgement on. The other scripts I have looked at do not enable me to come to any unequivocal conclusion. But the tendencies, in my opinion, are at least suggestive and these are what I shall now focus on.

2.1. Concord

One of the typical language problems I looked at, without expecting it to reveal anything significant since it does not reflect Danish influence, was concord. Here, out of 58 candidates (who, between them, dealt with seven different articles) 35 made at least one mistake of concord (21 : one mistake; 14 : two or more). Of these 35, only seven made mistakes in the passage set for translation. Moreover, one of these mistakes was probably one that the candidate had thought about (it was the only mistake he made): '... one would think that as an American who *have* lived and worked here for 18 years I ought to feel flattered'. It is possible that the candidate, whose general level of proficiency was high, thought that 'who' related to 'I', and not to 'an American'. I was surprised to find that there were comparatively few mistakes of concord in the translation and tentatively conclude that here the candidates paid particular attention to this feature. In fact, generally speaking concord does not separate the sheep from the goats: several of the students with an otherwise excellent command of the language made one or two mistakes in this area, whereas some of the students who failed (and deservedly so) made none at all.

2.2. Spelling

Spelling is another area which I did not expect to be significant, and in this case I was right. If a candidate had problems with spelling, the mistakes were distributed more or less evenly throughout his script. Most of the mistakes can, predictably, be attributed to interference from Danish (e.g. 'succesful', 'fysical' and 'litterature'). Thus one student wrote 'profet' (for 'prophet') in her essay, but two sentences earlier almost got the far less frequent 'prophylaxis' right: her version was 'prophylaxsis' - here interference did not affect the 'ph', but must have been responsible for the intrusive 's'. Only in one instance could the translation passage be blamed for a spelling mistake: one student translated *nabolandene* (twice) by 'nabouring countries', but spelt 'neighbourhood' correctly in the essay.

In what follows I shall be discussing examples taken from the 34 examination scripts that I have examined in some detail.

2.3. Word Order

Many Danish students still have problems with word order, particularly the position of adverbs in subordinate clauses (it is here, too, that native English speakers seem to make most mistakes of word order in Danish). A scrutiny of the 34 scripts revealed seven mistakes of this nature and a sprinkling of other types, but altogether fewer than I had anticipated. However, in some instances it seems as if the mistakes could be attributed directly to the influence of the Danish text.

Thus in the summary one student incorporated a modified version of a sentence from the Danish article: 'Og enten har danskerne ikke opdaget det, eller også er de åbenbart revnende ligeglade', which she rendered as: 'Either has this passed unnoticed or the Danes don't care'. She made no other mistakes of word order at all and her sentence structure was complex enough for her to have done so.

Another student produced three mistakes of word order in the translation:

Here should the family and the peer group support each other
(Her bør familie- og kammeratskabsgruppen gensidigt støtte hinanden)

when the child or children no longer are so dependent
(efterhånden som barnet eller børnene ikke længere er så afhængige)

For all the members of the family it is hard to find the balance ...
(For alle familiens medlemmer er det svært at finde balancen ...)

Admittedly, the last example cannot be classified as a mistake, but it would be far more natural to say: 'It is hard for all the members of the family ...' or 'All the members of the family find it hard to strike the balance ...' This student made only one other mistake of word order, this being in the essay: '... that the question hardly can be answered', but she got the word order right in all other subordinate clauses, e.g. 'that she was never going to recover / because you will always think ...'.

Another translation text was also responsible for a mistake of inversion (which is the most serious mistake among those quoted above): 'Allerede da han var 18 år, havde han solgt sin første historie', which was rendered by one student as: 'Already when he was 18 years old had he sold his first story'. This sentence contained the only mistakes of word order that this student made; in the essay, for instance, she produced structures like: 'After all, I think that most of us need to get away from our daily routine, because no matter what we do for a living the novelty is bound to wear off at some stage'.

The above sentence: 'Allerede da han var 18 år, havde han solgt sin første historie' proved to be a stumbling block for eight of the twelve candidates who dealt with this text. Six of them placed 'already' with 'when he was 18 / at the age of 18'; two of them omitted it, and changed the tense, ending up with the wrong meaning: 'When he was 18, he sold his first story'. (I would suggest: 'By the time he was 18, he had already sold his first story' as the most suitable rendering.) Certain Danish structures containing *allerede* always pose problems, and here Vinterberg and Bodelsen's *Dansk Engelsk Ordbog* is not helpful, containing as it does the (rare?) example 'already 200 years ago', which leads students to assume that 'already' can be combined with any adverbial of time. However, since none of these students used 'already' elsewhere in their papers, I have no way of knowing whether they would use it correctly if they were not translating.

2.4. The definite article

There is a tendency for Danish students to overuse the definite article in English, this reflecting the fact that Danish and English seem to have slightly different conceptions of what constitutes generic as opposed to specific reference. 16 of the 34 candidates had problems with the definite article, typical mistakes, which seem hard to eradicate, being 'U.S.A.' (i.e. without the definite article) and 'the society'. Other mistakes, however, seem to have their origin in the Danish text.

One of the articles deals with popular literature in the shape of female romances, and there are constant references to *triviallitteratur / trivial-litteraturen* and *kiosklitteratur / kiosklitteraturen*. This caused five of the twelve candidates to refer to 'the trivial / kiosk / popular literature' in either the summary or the essay (the word does not occur in the translation). In one instance, it was only when the candidate incorporated a sentence from the article into her summary that she misused the definite article: 'He even compares the trivial literature with pollution' ('Man kan betragte kiosk-litteraturen som en slags åndelig forurening'); otherwise she correctly referred to 'trivial literature' (except for the fact that 'trivial' can be disputed!). She also put: 'the reality cannot compete' ('virkeligheden slet ikke kan konkurrere'), but in the essay she wrote about 'real life' without using the article.

Again, one of the two mistakes that another student made in the summary can be directly traced to the article itself: 'the perfect love' ('den totale kærlighed'), and the other indirectly, 'the women and the young girls are attracted ...' ('den store gruppe af læsere er de helt unge piger. Men så har vi også de kvinder, der gerne vil blive ved med at være unge piger'). The latter example seems on the face of it dubious, but can be defended inasmuch as this student made no other such mistakes in either the summary or a long and competently written essay that contained abundant opportunities for misusing the definite article.

A similar example occurred in connection with another article, in which a student wrote 'the puberty' (*puberteten*) in the translation and 'the life belongs to the individual' in the essay, this being an acknowledged quotation from the article ('livet er personens eget'), but otherwise made no mistakes of this kind, using e.g. 'society', 'life', 'reality' correctly without the definite article.

2.5. Aspect

Both the progressive aspect and the distinction between the present perfect and the preterite tend to pose problems for Danish students. Only one student - out of the 34 - had problems with the present perfect as opposed to the preterite, largely, perhaps, because none of the five articles made it necessary to distinguish between the two in either the translation or the summary.

There were, on the other hand, 22 mistakes (made by 16 students) relating to the progressive aspect, 17 of them occurring in the present tense, where the tendency was to overuse it. A few students used it too little, thus making mistakes in either the summary or the translation in connection with one of the articles, where it was necessary to use the present progressive. However, if a student did make mistakes, it seemed to have rather less to do with the Danish text than with the student's grasp of this particular grammatical area.

2.6. *Nogle* / some

A much rarer mistake was definitely engendered by the Danish text. One of the translation passages contained the following sentence: 'Jeg blev mest optaget af det Danmark, jeg flyttede til for 18 år siden, på grund af nogle danske æstetiske værdier og egenskaber og nogle traditioner, som var "typisk danske".' This particular sentence produced some most peculiar renderings: 'I was most taken in by the Denmark I moved to' / 'What occupied me the most' / 'when I moved to it' / 'ethic values' / 'Danish properties' and five instances of 'typical Danish'. What surprised me, though, was that as many as seven out of eight students translated *nogle* by 'some', and I concluded that this was unthinking direct translation, especially as one of the seven wrote in her summary: 'When she first came to Denmark *certain* cultural features fascinated her'. 'Certain' would, I think, have been the best word to render *nogle*.

In all the translation passages, there were, of course, sentences, clauses or lexical items that created problems in the context. I shall now look at some of the more interesting examples, interesting in so far as the same features occurred in the summary and / or essay.

2.7. *Man / det*

One of the articles dealt with the hypothesis that people's behaviour can be affected by their diet. One of the sentences to be translated ran as follows: 'Ligeledes har man i mange fængsler ændret fangernes kost, fordi man tror, at det nedsætter volden blandt de indsatte'. Further on in the text we find: 'I enhver skole kan man finde børn, som er så aktive, at det grænser til det neurotiske'. Admittedly, only five candidates (out of twelve) worked on this article, but I used this text with a class of students the following year, and the results were comparable.

There turned out to be two difficulties: rendering *man* and *det*, both of which constitute recurrent problems for many Danish students. Two of the candidates produced acceptable renderings along the following lines: 'Similarly, in many prisons the prisoners' diet has been changed, because it is believed that this will reduce violence among the inmates'.

One candidate put: 'Many prisons have changed the prisoners' diet because they believe that it reduces violence', which changes the meaning completely (six of the students who did the translation for homework produced something similar). This candidate used 'it' wrongly in both the summary and the essay, and had problems with cohesion in general.

Another candidate wrote: 'It has been attempted in various prisons to change the prisoners' eating habits, because it is believed that it will decrease violence', which is an inaccurate translation, but does not change the meaning. However, 'it will decrease violence' is wrong, and this candidate, too, repeatedly used 'it' in the wrong context in the essay.

The fifth candidate had: 'Many jails have changed their menus (!) because they believe that it reduces violence ...'. Yet she demonstrated in both the summary and the essay that she could use both 'it' and 'this' in the correct context, making no mistakes at all.

None of these students seemed to have problems with using the various English equivalents of the Danish *man* in either the summary or the essay (i.e. 'you', 'one', 'they', 'people', passive or impersonal constructions, depending on the context).

Only one candidate produced a reasonable rendering of the second sentence: 'In every school you can find children who are so active that they are close to being neurotic' ('I enhver skole kan man finde børn, som er så aktive, at det grænser til det neurotiske'). The other four all put variations of: 'that it borders on the neurotic'. Two of them had no mistakes involving 'it' in the summary and essay.

Teachers of English - especially, perhaps, at advanced level - are aware that there is a tendency for Danes to overuse 'it' in English. This tendency was certainly confirmed by a number of the other examination scripts, although this particular feature was not tested in the other translation texts. It is difficult to generalize from the five candidates who had to translate *det*, but it would seem that translation is at least likely to generate mistakes in the use of 'it'.

2.8. Vocabulary

A section of the text about female romances also led to dubious renderings which in general do not occur elsewhere in the students' scripts: 'Erling Poulsens romaner er oftest bygget efter samme opskrift. Han har endda lavet 25 gyldne råd om, hvordan man skærer en sådan historie'.

Nine out of twelve candidates translated *en sådan historie* by 'such a story'; two put 'a story like that' which, in the context, was not acceptable either; the twelfth candidate had 'this kind of story', which is in my opinion the best solution. Only one of the candidates used 'such a' in a similar construction elsewhere, whereas several of them used 'this kind of'.

Needless to say, *25 gyldne råd* produced '25 golden advice / advises', but only in two instances. (However, later on in the translation passage four candidates wrote 'his 24th golden advice'.) Five students put '25 golden pieces of advice', but in the summary three of them used the idiomatic expression '25 golden rules'. The question is why they did not use this expression in the translation, as '25 golden pieces of advice' (or, perhaps more correctly: '25 pieces of golden advice') is a decidedly clumsy rendering. The explanation could be that 'golden rules' is a translation of *gyldne regler*, and they wanted to demonstrate that they knew 'pieces of advice'. I would suggest 'golden hints' as an adequate and more elegant rendering.

In the same translation text, the word *romanforfatter* appears. Only four of the candidates translated it correctly by 'novelist'. The others used: 'writer / author / romance writer' and, in three cases, 'novel writer'(!). There was no need to use 'novelist' in the summary, where all of them put 'writer' or 'author', but in the essay one of the three who had produced 'novel writer' employed the term 'novelist' instead.

I have come across other instances of this kind of mental block in the translation, with the correct word or expression cropping up in either the essay or the summary. One such instance is 'han er meget velformuleret', which one student, who had an excellent command of English, translated by 'he formulates his words well'. Yet in the summary he described this person as being 'eloquent', which would have been a vast improvement on 'he formulates his words well' (although not so good as 'articulate').

Another student used 'youngster' and 'young people' correctly in both the summary and the essay, but in the translation, which necessitated rendering *ungen* and *de unge*, he wrote 'the young' and 'youngs'. (He failed.) Such examples could be duplicated, but enough is enough.

2.9. Restructuring

The examples of Danish I have given may seem too elementary and therefore not sufficiently challenging for students at this level. Of course, the translation passages also contained structures that had to be changed considerably in order to function in English. However, such structures can be changed in various ways and are therefore not so susceptible to the kind of comparative analysis that I have been attempting to carry out. I am aware, though, that it is necessary to perform such analyses, and to take account of sentence structure altogether, in order to arrive at a more complete picture of a given student's performance in translation on the one hand and free production on the other.

3. Conclusion

Someone once said to me, in a tone of utter contempt, that 'linguistic research is easy; it just involves counting!' Even if this were true, one still has to know what to count and what the implications are. And here I am very much aware that what I have counted does not amount to a great deal, either in terms of the features themselves or as regards the number of students responsible for them. The ability to write good English is not synonymous with the ability to use the definite article correctly, to place adverbs in the correct position or to avoid making mistakes of concord. Writing skills begin when these elementary features are under control. But it so happened that these features were those that most easily lent themselves to a preliminary investigation of this nature. My findings, slender as they are, suggest, at least to me, that a translation exercise does not necessarily give a convincing picture of a student's ability to cope with, for instance, linguistic features that represent a contrast between the two languages. It would seem that in some instances the source language, which confronts the student in black and white, intervenes to such an extent that he translates directly, without having recourse to the whole of his knowledge of the target language. He is, then, very often thinking and working in the source language rather than rethinking and reworking the text in the foreign language into which he is translating. In other words, the skills and techniques that are required when one translates are somewhat different from those that are necessary when one writes directly in the foreign language. I am not suggesting that translation in no way reflects the translator's ability to write in the foreign language - that would be ridiculous and counter to what any foreign language teacher has observed for himself. What I am suggesting is that a translation by no means gives a complete or reliable picture.

For one thing, writing is only partially related to what is normally called 'language proficiency'. The ability to write well requires the marshalling of a range of different skills, some of which have little to do with language proficiency *per se*. These include the selection of the necessary points, facts or arguments, the organization of these in a coherent and cohesive text, and the employment of an appropriate style. Style is an important factor in translating, but the translator is not expected to create his own coherence or his own argumentation. Thus his ability to produce a text - and this is surely what we mean by the ability to write - is not fully tested. (Having said that, I will admit that it is perfectly possible for a bad translation to destroy either the coherence or the cohesion of the source text; this was demonstrated in the example above, where students used 'it' and 'they' incorrectly).

For another thing, a translation text does not always give the examinee an opportunity to demonstrate his ability to exploit the foreign language. He is bound by the structures and vocabulary of the source language text, and these may be restricted or totally alien to a style in which he excels. Added to this, examination texts vary considerably; some of them 'test' some linguistic features, others completely different ones. The translation passages that we have set over the years are a case in point. And how should the examiner react to lexical items that reflect the candidate's wide vocabulary, but which deviate from the style of the translation text? In the text about female romances, the word *hovedperson* occurs, and this two or three of the better candidates translated as 'protagonist'. This is a perfectly good word; but it stuck out like a sore thumb in the context, where 'main character' was the appropriate expression.

In my opinion, there can be no doubt that translation is an important and useful component of any advanced foreign language course. It is a valuable adjunct to the teaching of language proficiency, it is a technique which all advanced language students should become acquainted with, it is a skill which, once acquired, will stand many language graduates in good stead. I am just not convinced that it is the best test of the ability to write in English. As to what the best test is, well, that was not the subject of this article.

Notes

1. Christine Klein-Braley and Veronica Smith, 1985. 'Incalculable and full of risks?: Translation L1 to L2 as a testing procedure' in Christopher Titford and Adolf E. Hieke eds.: *Translation in foreign language teaching and testing*. Tubingen: Narr, 155-168.
2. Robert Lado, 1961. *Language testing: the construction and use of foreign language tests - A teacher's book*. London: Longman, Green and Co.; New York; McGraw-Hill. Quoted by Klein-Braley and Smith (1985:158).
3. G. Collier and B. Shields, 1977. *Guided German-English translation*. Heidelberg: Quelle Meyer. Quoted by Klein-Braley and Smith (1985:158).
4. I have included this example because the discrepancy between the candidate's English in the translation passage and the other two sections is so striking. What my preliminary investigation has revealed, however, is that students tend to make more mistakes of certain types in translation than in free production. In other words, this particular candidate does not seem to be typical.

Computer Aided Translation

Viggo Hjørnager Pedersen
Helene Bekker-Nielsen Dunbar

Machine translation is far from being a new concept.[1] Research has been going on since the late 1940's and by now there are several main-frame translation systems on the market, such as METAL, Systran, Logos, ATLAS, HICATS, TAURUS, LMT, Rosetta, MU-2, JFY-IV, ODA, and CUM-MT.[2] Some of these programs only translate within very tightly defined limits. One example of this type of system is PACE (Perkins Approved Clear English) where each word can only have one meaning, while the length of the sentence is kept as short as possible and all but simple grammatical forms are avoided. Within these limits PACE works. Other systems such as EUROTRA can handle complex grammar, but are unfortunately very slow.[3]

A program which will translate a text into clear, concise prose is still a thing of the future. None of the available programs are able to take contextual matters into consideration so as to render the implicit meaning of the text. This, of course, is a limitation which will only disappear with the 'thinking' computer.

In order to get a decent translation, there has to be interaction between the machine and the operator. This concept is called Computer Aided Translation (CAT). The operator uses the program to provide quick translations of words, phrases and special terminology, but has to post-edit the translation to get an acceptable text. CAT is possible on main-frame, mini, and PC systems. On the one hand, main-frame and mini systems have the advantage of being very big (but expensive) systems which can hold an enormous amount of data, whereas PCs are more limited in their storage capacity. On the other hand, PC systems have the advantage of being cheap and are thus within the reach of free-lance translators. It must be remembered that the size of a PC depends on the size of its disk capacity and the speed of the disk. At the moment the disk capacity is doubling every couple of years, which means that every new version of a PC is bigger, better, and cheaper than its predecessor.

At present there are two PC translation systems on the Danish market. One is PC Translator, the other is Winger 92. Both work on the basic principle that it is possible to translate phrases with phrases, words with words. This can, of course, give some problems, as a word may have several different lexical meanings or grammatical functions. This is why the operator has to translate interactively. The operator decides which words to use where, corrects grammar, and makes sure that contextual matters are taken into consideration in the translation.

We have decided to concentrate on Winger 92 in this article for two reasons. One is that PC Translator has already been described and analysed by Søren Juul Nielsen (1988). The other is that Winger 92 is a newly developed program which has only just come onto the market and which is based on a new type of database.

Winger 92 is based on a Reduced Information Databasestructure (RID), which is a new way of storing words. It offers fast random access and compresses the data to a high degree. The size of the database develops logarithmically (see Figure 1), i.e. the number of characters stored in the index will always be smaller than or equal to the number of symbols in the keys, if the number of keys is smaller than the alphabet. If more keys are stored than the number of symbols in the alphabet, then the number of symbols in the RID index will always be smaller than the total number of symbols in the keys.[4] In other words, the number of extra letters stored for each new entry is dependent on the number of words already stored in the database, e.g.

ban<u>an</u> = banana
ban<u>egård</u> = station
banegård<u>en</u> = the station
bane<u>mand</u> = railwayman

where the database structure only stores the differences between the words. In the case of *banegård*, *banegården*, and *banemand* it first stores *ban* and then *egård*, *en*, and *mand*. When *banan* is inserted, it only stores *an* and so forth. On average each new entry means 3.4 letters more. This means that even though a lot of data is put into the database, it is still possible to get access to it quickly, and it does not take up much space on the hard disk.

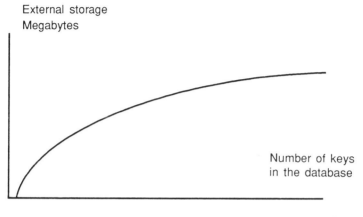

(Ib Elfving, 1989).

Figure 1. Graph showing the extension of the RID database

When the program is running, it breaks up the sentences into single words or phrases. Then the words and phrases are compared with the words and phrases in the database, after which corresponding forms are replaced. Phrases always take precedence over words, so phrasal verbs, set expressions, etc. are always translated as such and not as single words. As the database is practically unlimited, there is enough space to store special terminologies, set expressions and phrases covering the most common grammatical problems. The program itself does not have any in-built grammar. It is of course self-evident that the larger the database becomes the slower it gets, but as it sorts and replaces within microseconds, this is not a problem.[5]

PC translation systems are interactive, which means that the operator can add whatever phrases or words he wants to the database. By running frequency tests on different types of texts, the operator can define and determine his terminology and adapt the database accordingly. To give an example of this we only have to think of the translator translating computer manuals. Computer manuals are all more or less alike, as they all employ the present tense, have short sentences, and use a very limited vocabulary. The translator can update the database with the terminology required, together with the most common phrases, and in this way save time and work when translating.

111

As mentioned above, Winger 92 works by comparing phrases with phrases, words with words. There are several minor problems, which should be rectified, as these problems can become a nuisance to the operator. One problem is that the program does not translate figures, which means that the operator has to post-edit all figures. This is mainly a problem when translating financial texts, where Danish currency figures (e.g. kr. 123.990,00) are translated into Danish/English (DDK. 123.990,00) instead of English (DDK. 123,990.00). It might be argued that this is a very minor problem, but it can be rather irritating to have to post-edit so much in a finished text, when one knows that a very small addition to the program could eliminate the problem. A second problem is that even though the program can translate texts in WordPerfect 5.0 format and make a WordPerfect 5.0 file of the finished text, it has problems coping with the WordPerfect codes. This has the effect of breaking up words and phrases with the result that the program cannot recognise and translate them. These are just two of the problems that we have had working with Winger 92. We do not believe that these problems are confined to the one program, but rather that the real core of the problem lies in the fact that PC translation programs are written by programmers without the necessary linguistic knowledge, to be used by linguists without the necessary technical knowledge. The more widespread PC translation programs become, the greater is the chance that cooperation between linguists and programmers can take place and result in better programs.

Winger 92

Winger 92 comes with a Danish-English and an English-Danish word list. Each comprises about 90,000 entries and can be extended. In theory the database can be extended almost indefinitely and in practice nobody knows how much can actually be contained in it. Each entry equals a word or a phrase. This does not mean that there are 90,000 different words and phrases, but rather that each word or phrase exists in several forms, for example:

night	nat
a night	en nat
nights	nætter
last night	i aftes
tomorrow night	i morgen aften
all night	hele natten

Within the program it is possible to 'teach' the database new words by using a function called 'learn new words' (F2). It is thus possible to insert words or phrases in the forms that occur most frequently in the type of work the operator usually translates, if they do not already exist in the database. This can be done by making a word list as an ASCII file and reading it directly into the database to update, change or extend the database.

To initiate the translation of a text the operator starts off by selecting the language combination, at the moment Danish-English or English-Danish. Then he indicates what type of input file (source text) he has. This can either be an ASCII file, a WordPerfect 5.0 file or the text typed directly from the keyboard. After this he selects the output file, again either as ASCII, if the input file is ASCII or directly typed, WordPerfect 5.0, if the input file is WordPerfect 5.0, or the screen, and starts the translation. If the operator produces a WordPerfect 5.0 output file, then it cannot be post-edited within the Winger 92 program.

When the program is running, the screen consists of two big windows, one with the source text and one with the translation, and a blank space where additional windows come up as they are needed (see Figure 2.). The two texts run concurrently, so that the operator can read the source text and the translation and compare.

The menu in the translation window has the same functions as the function keys. This is also where the operator selects parameters.

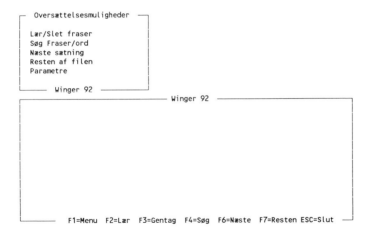

(F1=Menu, F2=Learn, F3=Repeat, F4=Search, F6=Next sentence F7=In batch, ESC=End)

Figure 2. The translation window

113

There are two ways of translating a text. Either the operator translates in batch (F7) or he translates interactively. When the text is translated in batch, unknown words are put in brackets [ ] and alternative translations of the same source language form (e.g. Danish *selv* = 'even/self', English 'bank' = *bred*/*bank*) are put in left and right angle brackets < >. To run the program interactively the operator has to choose parameters beforehand. These parameters give the operator several choices. He can choose to insert unknown words as they occur, he can choose to select alternative translations as they come up on the screen, and he can choose whether he wants to have the source text included in the output file sentence by sentence, so as to ease comparison. If the operator chooses to insert unknown words as they occur, the translation will stop every time the program cannot 'recognise' a word. As it only recognises phrases if they are in the database in exactly the same form as in the source text, the program will not stop and ask for translation of phrases. Therefore, inserting new words one by one as the translation progresses is only a good idea in cases where many single words (e.g. technical terms) are unknown. It is better to wait and identify complete phrases (e.g. *Vi anerkender modtagelsen af Deres brev af:* 'we acknowledge receipt of your letter of'). Choosing between alternative translations as the translation progresses can be useful, but as the same function exists in the editing program it seems rather redundant.

When the text is translated interactively, the operator makes the decisions while the program is running. He has to use the function F6 (translation sentence by sentence), as this is the only way to check the translation while running the program. Once a sentence has been translated by the program it is not possible to scroll back to a previous sentence, if the operator wishes to ensure that the translation is consistent. After having worked with the program we have reached the conclusion that the most time-saving and least stressful way of translating is by using sentence by sentence mode (F6), inserting unknown words and phrases in each sentence (F2), and then repeating the sentence to see if the result is reasonable (F3).

While in the translation program, it is possible to search through the database to see which words and phrases are already inserted. If the operator knows that he has 'taught' the database a certain phrase, but cannot remember the exact wording, he can make the program search (F4) through the database and write all the words or phrases in a window by typing in the first part of the phrase or word. Thus if the operator wants to see how he usually translates the phrase 'we thank you for your letter of', he types in 'we', presses F4, and gets all the phrases and words which start with the letter combination 'we' with their translations.

In the post-editing mode (see Figure 3) the operator can insert capital letters (which do not always occur in the same places in the two languages), choose between alternative translations, and change sentence structures. Here it is also possible to disregard the existing alternative translations and insert a new translation without storing it in the database. This can be an advantage with very specialized terminologies, where there can be words which are generally used in one sense, but which are used in a very specific sense in certain circumstances.

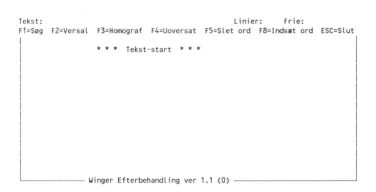

(F1=Search, F2=Capital, F3=Alternative translations, F4=Unknown word,
F5=Delete, F8=Insert word, ESC=End)

Figure 3. The post-editing window.

Some examples of Winger 92 Computer Aided Translation

When the operator has translated a source text he can put it into a file (either ASCII or WordPerfect) and print it from there. If the operator has not selected alternative translations before printing, all alternative translations are printed within right and left angle brackets < >.

On the following page is a short translation of a text from English into Danish.[6] The text has been translated in batch mode. The database in this case comprises about 90,000 entries from English to Danish.

Text 1a

Doctors can now find out in a minute whether patients with bulimia, or compulsive overeating, are trying to conceal their behaviour. A simple blood test will determine if patients are engaging in bingeing followed by vomiting.

According to Harry Gwirtsman, of the school of medicine at the University of California, Los Angeles, doctors need such a test because bulimics are almost always surreptitious and deny such behaviour.

Læger kan nu <opfatte/finde> ud [in] <en/et> minut hvorvidt patienter med bulimi eller tvingende fylderi, prøver på at gemme deres opførsel. <en/et> enkel blodprøve <vil/skal> afgøre <hvis/om> patienter giver sig af med orgier efterfulgt af opkastninger. Ifølge [Harry] [Gwirtsman], [of] skolen [of] medicin [at] <den/det> Universitet [of] Californien, Los Angeles, læger <behov/behøver> sådan en test fordi [bulimics] er næsten altid hemmelighedsfulde og benægte sådan opførsel.

As can be seen, the program has problems coping with gender distinctions (neuter and common gender) which exist in Danish. This is apparent in the construction 'a minute' = *et minut*, where the noun *minut* is neuter and takes the indefinite article *et*, and in the construction 'a simple blood test' = *en enkel blodprøve*, where *blodprøve* is common gender and takes the indefinite article *en*. If the noun *blodprøve* had been neuter, then the adjective *enkel* would be *enkelt*, plural *enkle*. Nor can the program manage the difference in sentence structure between Danish and English, where English always has normal word order in statements, while Danish has inversion if the sentence starts with an adverbial phrase, an adverb, an object or a clause. Another very difficult point is prepositions, which because of their many possible translations are better left untranslated, unless they can be translated as part of a phrase. These problems can to a certain extent be circumvented by the use of phrases, for instance in the case of gender. The problem with this solution is that it only works in some cases and not in all, and thus leaves a vast amount of post-editing.

To show how much the use of phrases can help to solve these grammatical problems, we have inserted the relevant phrases into the database and translated the text in batch (Text 1b).

The phrases are:

find out = *finde ud af*
in a minute = *på et minut*

a simple blood test = *en almindelig blodprøve*
will determine = *kan afgøre*
the school of medicine = *det medicinske fakultet*
the University of California = *University of California*
bulimics = *bulimi-patienter*
such behaviour = *en sådan opførsel*
compulsive overeating = *sygelig trang til at spise for meget*

Text 1b

> Læger kan nu finde ud af på et minut hvorvidt patienter med bulimi, eller sygelig trang til at spise for meget, prøver på at gemme deres opførsel. En almindelig blodprøve kan afgøre <hvis/om> patienter giver sig af med orgier efterfulgt af opkastninger. Ifølge [Harry] [Gwirtsman], [of] det medicinske fakultet [at] University of California, Los Angeles, læger behøver sådan en test fordi bulimi-patienter er næsten altid hemmelighedsfulde og benægte en sådan opførsel.

The inclusion of more phrases has made the text into somewhat better Danish. The problem of inversion in Danish clauses still exists and will as long as the program is unintelligent. This can, of course, also be remedied with phrases, but would then interfere with cases where Danish does not have inversion. The objection that can, of course, be made to the method of translating by means of phrases added during revision is that it is very time-consuming. However, as the system is primarily designed to translate standard texts within restricted terminologies, updating the program will rapidly lead to real and lasting improvement of performance.

Text 1b is still a rough translation which needs some editing. This is done in the editing program, (or in WordPerfect, if the output file is a WordPerfect file). Post-editing involves choosing between alternative translations, re-phrasing expressions, changing sentence structures, inserting capital letters and punctuation. Text 1c is the edited result of Text 1b.

Text 1c

> Læger kan nu på et minut finde ud af hvorvidt patienter med bulimi, eller sygelig trang til at spise for meget, prøver på at skjule deres opførsel. En almindelig blodprøve kan afgøre om patienterne hengiver sig til orgier efterfulgt af opkastninger. Ifølge Harry Gwirtsman fra det medicinske fakultet, University of California i Los Angeles, behøver lægerne en sådan test, da bulimi-patienter næsten altid er hemmelighedsfulde og benægter en sådan opførsel.

Some of the problems solved here - and some of those not solved - will probably remain the province of human post-editors for some time to come, even with more advanced programs. Thus English indefinite to Danish definite (doctors = *lægerne*) will be extremely difficult to cope with, as the English indefinite form must sometimes be preserved and sometimes be changed in translation. Improving *på et minut* (line 1) to *på et øjeblik* would be easy, if the latter was added as an extra translation. But it will not do to leave too many alternatives for the post-editor.

When translating from Danish into English a number of different grammatical problems arise. Text 2[7] has been translated in the same way as Text 1. The Danish-English word list consists of about 120,000 entries.

Text 2

Skriveskræk og præsentations-angst. Selv trænede skribenter kan pludselig opleve angsten for det hvide papir - eller den tomme skærm - og mere end en student har trukket specialstudiet i langdrag. Men hvorfor er det svært at skrive?	Fear of writing and dread of achievement. Self coached writers can sudden experience the fear of <the/it/that/so> white paper - or <the/that/it> <empty/inch> screen - and more than one student <has/have> pulled the thesis writing for a long time. But why it is difficult <that/to> write?

The grammatical problems arising from translating Danish into English are concord, expanded tenses, and sentence structures. Some of these problems can again be remedied by the use of phrases, for instance concord in the case of personal pronouns in the 1st and 2nd persons, singular and plural. The obvious solution to most of these problems is to create alternative translations (for instance simple and expanded tenses) and thus delete rather than correct. Lexical problems are (relatively) high frequency items with many possible translations like *selv*, and verbal phrases with embedded obects like *trukket specialstudiet i langdrag* from *trække i langdrag*. *Selv* can be an adverb, corresponding to 'even', as in the text above, or a reflexive pronoun, in which case there are many possible translations: *selv ville hun (han, I, de, etc) ikke sige noget* = 'she (he, you, they, etc) would not say anything herself (himself, yourselves, themselves, etc)'. The best solution here as with the prepositions is to leave '*selv*' untranslated for the post-editor to cope with. Text 2b shows the result if we decide to include a few phrases. We have added

er det = is it[8]
den tomme skærm = the empty screen
det hvide papir = the white paper
trænede = trained/experienced

> Fear of writing and dread of achievement.
> [Selv] <trained/experienced> writers can sudden experience the fear of the white paper - or the empty screen - and more than one student <has/have> pulled the thesis writing for a long time. But why <it is/is it> difficult to write?

Text 2c is the edited result of Text 2b. We have decided between the alternative translations, changed the adjective 'sudden' to the adverbial 'suddenly', found an ad hoc solution for *trække i langdrag*, and corrected the sentence structure.

> Fear of writing and dread of achievement.
> Even experienced writers can suddenly experience the fear of the white paper - or the empty screen - and more than one student has made slow progress with his thesis. But why is it difficult to write?

Comparison with PC Translator

PC Translator has been tested and described by Søren Juul Nielsen. In the following we shall compare our findings with his to highlight the advantages and disadvantages of the systems. Since Søren Juul Nielsen's description of PC Translator, a new version has come onto the market, which has not yet been described. In the following we use the term 'word list' to describe the dictionaries in the programs. We have decided to do this, as neither of the two programs have got dictionaries in the proper lexical sense of the word; they simply list possible translations without explanation or exemplification.

One of the main differences between PC Translator and Winger 92 is in the use of the database. PC Translator has three word lists: a general list which comes with the program and which consists of 80,000 entries, a user word list which the operator builds, and a phrase list which the operator can edit and expand (Nielsen, 1988:12-22). Other differences between the two systems consist of an automatic syntax function (PC Translator), the size of the word lists, where Winger 92 has a bigger database, the size of the programs with the databases (Winger 92 3.5 MB, PC Translator 3.0 MB), and the operator interfaces.

In PC Translator the general word list cannot be edited by the operator. This word list consists of single words, where each word has one translation. The user word list can be edited from the translation program and is intended for special terminologies. The phrase list can be edited in a word processing program outside PC Translator. In the version Søren Juul Nielsen tested there was room for 230 different phrases before the phrase list was full.

PC Translator works by translating sentence by sentence. First it compares with the phrase list, then the user word list and finally with the general word list. Words which do not exist in either of the three lists are not translated but written in the source language. PC Translator mainly works in batch, i.e. without interaction from the user (Nielsen, 1988:5-6).

Winger 92 only operates with one word list. It is possible to insert and delete words and phrases in this word list from the program. Like PC Translator, Winger 92 compares the source text with the word list, the longest phrases being translated first. The most satisfactory way of using Winger 92 is by working interactively.

The main limitation of PC Translator in the version described by Søren Juul Nielsen is the limited scope of the phrase list, which most translators will find too small. However, it seems that the new version of the program has overcome this problem. In contrast to Winger 92, PC Translator has some in-built grammar; however, as demonstrated by Søren Juul Nielsen, it is still very far from being able to analyse a sentence so as to produce a correct translation. In addition, the quality of the general word list leaves much to be desired, and it is inconvenient that it is not possible to get rid of misleading or wrong translations in it.

The main drawback of Winger 92 is its total lack of grammar. However, a new version is under way which is intended to partially overcome this deficiency. Meanwhile, the main attraction of the system is its ability to accommodate large numbers of new words and phrases, and the ease with which the first rough draft can be manipulated.

Conclusion

Machine translation on PCs is still a very new idea. As the size of the PC determines how big a program can be, there is a limit to how good these programs can ever become. Within the limits outlined above the programs work satisfactorily, but neither of the two programs are developed to such an extent that it is possible to use them for automatic translation. At the moment the translations are readable and convey the overall meaning of the source text, but as long as the programs translate phrase by phrase and word by word, the text produced can never be more than a rough draft which can aid a translator in his or her work. It is self-evident that the more an operator works with the program, the better the program becomes, as the phrase and word lists are expanded. Whether PC systems could ever be more than an aid for the translator is not a question that can be answered at the moment.

Notes

1. For a brief survey of the history of the discipline, see Pedersen (1987:167-84). For a fuller discussion, see Mounin (1964) on the early stages, and Sørensen (1984) and Slocum (1985) on more recent developments.
2. *Language International*, I: 6, 1989.
3. Demonstrationspapir, 2 Dec. 1988.
4. Ib Elfving: 'RID databasen - statistiske beregninger', Winger Consult Aps, January 1990.
5. 'Rapport om maskinel sprog-oversættelse', Winger Consult Aps, October 1989.
6. *New Scientist*, 9 September, 1989.
7. *Humanist*, Copenhagen University, 26 Oktober, 1989.
8. In most cases Danish inversion is translated into normal word order in English. In order to solve this grammatical problem, the database translates Danish inversion as English normal word order in all phrases. This solves most problems, except the few where English has inversion as well, as is the case in this text.

Bibliography

Elfving, Ib: 'RID databasen - statistiske beregninger', Winger Consult Aps, January 1990.
Eurotra Demonstrationspapir, 2 Dec. 1988.
Mounin, G.: *La machine à traduire*. Haag, 1964.
Nielsen, Søren Juul: *Vurdering af PC-Translator*, et EDB-program til automatisk oversættelse fra engelsk til dansk, Institut for Datalingvistik, Handelshøjskolen i København, nov. 1988.
Pedersen, V. H.: *Oversættelsesteori*, 3rd ed., København 1987.
'Rapport om maskinel sprog-oversættelse', Winger Consult Aps, okt. 1989.
Slocum, J.: 'A Survey of Machine Translation: Its History, Current Status, and Future Prospects', *Computational Linguistics*, 1, 1985.
Sørensen, H. S.: 'Maskinoversættelse', *Nyt fra Terminologiafdelingen* nr. 9, Handelshøjskolen i København, 1984.
'Ten Years of Translating and the Computer', *Language International*, I:6, 1989.
Togeby, Ole: 'Parsing Danish Text in EUROTRA', *Nordiske Datalingvistikdage og Symposium for datamatstøttet leksikografi og terminologi 1987. Proceedings*, Institut for Datalingvistik, Handelshøjskolen i København, marts 1988.

Titles of related interest from
AARHUS UNIVERSITY PRESS

Bodil Due
The Cyropaedia. Xenophon's Aims and Methods. 264 pages, hardbound. 162 DKK.

The *Cyropaedia*, "On the Education of Cyrus", was widely read in Antiquity and during the Renaissance, but today ranks among the least read of Xenophon's works. Nonetheless, it is still of prime importance as a source for the study of fourth-century Greek thought, and for Xenophon's views on morality, education, and the ethics of leadership.

Claudio Bogantes
La narrativa socialrealista en Costa Rica, 1900-1950. 356 pages, hardbound. 200 DKK.

Knud Lundbæk
The Traditional History of the Chinese Script from a Seventeenth Century Chinese Manuscript. Facsimile Edition with translation and commentary. 64 pages, A4 size, hardbound. 203 DKK.

Gabriele Kasper (editor)
Learning, Teaching and Communication in the Foreign Language Classroom. 224 pages, paperback. 146 DKK.

AARHUS UNIVERSITY PRESS
Aarhus University, DK-8000 Aarhus C, Denmark